4/-

EFC Wolfe.

12 FEB 1947

THE NEW TEMPLE SHAKESPEARE

Edited by M. R. Ridley, M.A.

THE MERRY WIVES
OF WINDSOR

by William Shakespeare

London: J. M. DENT & SONS LTD.
New York: E. P. DUTTON & CO. INC.

All rights reserved
Printed in Great Britain
by Morrison & Gibb Ltd., London and Edinburgh
and decorated by
Eric Gill
for
J. M. Dent & Sons Ltd.
Aldine House, Bedford St. London

Toronto	.	*Vancouver*
Melbourne	.	*Wellington*

First Published in this Edition 1935
Reprinted 1941, 1946

Editor's General Note

The Text. The editor has kept before him the aim of presenting to the modern reader the nearest possible approximation to what Shakespeare actually wrote. The text is therefore conservative, and is based on the earliest reliable printed text. But to avoid distraction (*a*) the spelling is modernised, and (*b*) a limited number of universally accepted emendations is admitted without comment. Where a Quarto text exists as well as the First Folio the passages which occur only in the Quarto are enclosed in square brackets [ ] and those which occur only in the Folio in brace brackets { }.

Scene Division. The rapid continuity of the Elizabethan curtainless production is lost by the 'traditional' scene divisions. Where there is an essential difference of place these scene divisions are retained. Where on the other hand the change of place is insignificant the scene division is indicated only by a space on the page. For ease of reference, however, the 'traditional' division is retained at the head of the page and in line numbering.

Notes. Passages on which there are notes are indicated by a † in the margin.

Punctuation adheres more closely than has been usual to the 'Elizabethan' punctuation of the early texts. It is often therefore more indicative of the way in which the lines were to be delivered than of their syntactical construction.

Glossaries are arranged on a somewhat novel principle, not alphabetically, but in the order in which the words or phrases occur. The editor is much indebted to Mr J. N. Bryson for his collaboration in the preparation of the glossaries.

Preface

The Text. In 1602 appeared a Quarto with the title-page,
A / Most pleasaunt and / excellent conceited Co- / medie, of Syr
Iohn Falstaffe, and the / merrie Wiues of *Windsor*. / Entermixed
with sundrie / variable and pleasing humors, of Syr *Hugh* / the
Welch Knight, Iustice *Shallow*, and his / wise Cousin M. *Slender*. /
With the swaggering vaine of Auncient / *Pistoll*, and Corporall
Nym. / By *William Shakespeare*. / As it hath bene diuers times
Acted by the right Honorable / my Lord Chamberlaines seruants.
Both before her / Maiestie, and elsewhere. / LONDON / Printed by
T. C. for Arthur Iohnson, and are to be sold at / his shop in Powles
Church-yard, at the signe of the / Flower de Leuse and the Crowne. /
1602. The problem of the relation of this text to that of the
1623 Folio, and of either of them to Shakespeare's original, is one
of the most fascinating in the whole of Shakespearean textual
research ; but it is also unhappily one of the most intricate and
elusive. Even to state the data in such a way that the reader
would be able to base his independent judgment upon them would
occupy disproportionate space, since they must be given in full
(ideally in nothing less than a parallel text). Where some features
seem to point to ' reporting,' some to ' adaptation,' some to ' revision,' any attempt at summary, however honest, seems to lead to
a distortion of the relative importance of the various indications.
After several attempts at such a summary, and an equal number of
failures, I conclude that the only thing to be done is to refer
the reader who is interested in the problem to three places
where he will find it set out and argued in full, to give the
summarised conclusions of two editors, and to draw attention

to one or two features of the texts which affect the reading of the play.

The problem has been argued by H. C. Hart (from a rigidly conservative standpoint) in the introduction to the Arden edition of the play (1904); by W. W. Greg (in full detail and with great clarity and acumen) in the type-facsimile of the Quarto in the Tudor and Stuart Library (1910); and (very brilliantly and somewhat conjecturally) by the New Cambridge editors (1921). Greg's notion of the history of the play is, very briefly, as follows. Shakespeare wrote the play in 1598 or thereabouts; this was the play substantially as we have it, except that the 'horse-stealing' plot was more prominent, and its thread was properly interwoven with the denouement. Some while later it was thought desirable to get rid of most of the horse-stealing plot; an 'adapter' was told off to conduct this operation, which involved recasting the last act, and while he was about it he produced two versions of that act, one for representation at court, one for the ordinary stage. The alterations were clumsily applied to the stage version, and the new last act substituted for the original. But the actors were slovenly in learning their new parts. The copy for the Quarto was produced 'out of his head' by the actor who had played the Host, who knew his own part well, the parts of other actors who were on the stage at the same time as himself adequately, and the rest of the play comparatively ill, the end of it, owing to the alterations, worst of all. The Folio represents the full stage version of the play as it rested after the adapter's activities, and with perhaps a few sporadic alterations by Shakespeare, as well as an odd change of a proper name. The New Cambridge editors' idea of the business is somewhat different. Shakespeare did indeed produce the play in a hurry to obey the Queen's orders, but he did not write it ' out of nothing.' He took an old play, probably *The Jealous Comedy*, which the Chamberlain's men had played in 1593, and refurbished it. This play had in it the horse-stealing plot, which at that time, owing to the unpopular activities of a certain Count Mümpelgart, had a topical appeal, and also a Euphuistical and Osrician hero. Shakespeare dispensed with almost all of the horse-stealing plot, and turned the hero as best he could into Falstaff, the transmutation being oddly incomplete. Shakespeare was working in a hurry, and also by the end was getting thoroughly tired, if not bored, and he left therefore various inconsistencies. Of the play at this stage of its development the Quarto is an incomplete and garbled version. The Folio represents 'a revision of the same manuscript which lies, at whatever remove, and however garbled and abridged, at the back of the Quarto version.'

These two views [1] illustrate at least the complexity of the problem; it will be observed also that they both throw doubt on the authenticity of the Folio as a whole, since we do not know who conducted the ' adaptation' and the ' revision.' However, we have to be content with what we have got, namely the Folio text, with the assurance that at any rate the great bulk of it is Shakespeare's play. The only practical problem which confronts the editor in producing a text is the extent to which the Quarto may be used to modify or amplify the Folio. Here opinions differ widely. An austere editor like Hart admits the Quarto only three times (and two of those reluctantly). ' The Quarto,' he says, ' appears upon sufferance, fenced in, in the three places referred to, by brackets.' (In fact he also admits one oath from Q with a note but no brackets, and a variant reading in the same line, III. iii. 53,

---

[1] There is a masterly examination of them, with an even larger dose than usual of his astringent sanity, in Sir Edmund Chambers' *William Shakespeare*.

with no comment at all.) The New Cambridge editors permit themselves, I am sure rightly, more freedom. No doubt the Quarto is a 'Bad Quarto,' but I am not clear that Hart sufficiently observed and allowed for the particular kind of badness it exhibits. He says himself that 'the bulk of it is surely Shakespeare's,' and the important fact is that it does not move at a constant level of mediocrity; if it did, one might readily enough dismiss it. But, on the contrary, when it is bad it is wildly bad, excising important passages completely or compressing into a sort of synopsis that would be unintelligible without the Folio; but where it is good (*i.e.* when the Host is about, and also in one or two speeches of Falstaff even in the absence of the Host) it is more than adequate, and I think may be legitimately drawn upon. In the text which follows the insertions from it are all indicated by square brackets. I have also, arbitrarily, but again I think legitimately, restored a number of the oaths of the Quarto. Wherever one compares a 'good' Quarto with the Folio one finds that the Folio has excised or watered down (though in very varying degrees in different plays) the oaths of the Quarto, and one may be reasonably certain that the same process took place here. The danger is, of course, that when one is dealing with a reported text one may be dealing with expletives that the actors inserted to taste, particularly in prose where the rhythm was no check; but the differences between F and Q are in this respect exactly similar to those observable elsewhere, and some of the oaths are so characteristic (notably Sir Hugh's), and give such an added flavour, that it seems too ascetic to leave them in the oblivion of the Quarto.

Date of Composition. The play is usually attributed to 1598, between 2 *Henry IV* and *Henry V*. Dr Leslie Hotson, in *Shakespeare* *versus Shallow* (1931) (which is full of interest on other topics), argues for 1596-7, and would put the first performance of the play at the Garter Feast at Westminster on 23rd April 1597.

There is a strong tradition, which there seems no reason to doubt, that the play was produced in a great hurry in obedience to a command of the Queen, who wished to see Falstaff in love.

Sources. The main claimant for the position of source for the play is a story, derived from Straparola, in Tarlton's *Newes out of Purgatorie* (1590), which may have formed the basis of the (hypothetical) earlier play on which *The Merry Wives* was perhaps founded, or may have been used by Shakespeare direct. And if we are determined to find the buck-basket we can perhaps feel that we have run it to ground in Giovanni Fiorentino's *Il Pecorone*. But to look for any specific source for such a well-worn theme as the concealment of the lover from the jealous husband seems a waste of time.

What Daniel describes as the ' Mümpelgart business ' is, though intrinsically amusing, more important for the textual history of the play than for the play as we have it, since it is connected with the now almost vanished horse-stealing sub-plot.

Duration of Action. There has been a great deal of trouble about this (mainly centring round III. v.), and there is no doubt confusion caused by hurry in composition or by unskilful adaptation for the stage, or by both. I do not think that the trouble is as serious as is sometimes made out. In III. iii. the Wives decide to send Mistress Quickly to Falstaff again, and at the end of III. iv. she says she has an errand. It is objected that she has had no opportunity to have the errand delivered to her. But in fact the ordinary reader or playgoer does not so minutely trouble himself (except in a particular type of play) with what exactly the characters are doing when they are out of his sight. In the second place it is assumed that at the beginning of III. v. Falstaff must have just come in from his ducking. No doubt it would be amusing to see Falstaff looking like a drowned puppy, but there is no reason why he should not still the next morning feel the need of allaying Thames water with sack. The difficulty that then remains is Mistress Quickly's remark at the end of III. iv., as to slacking the errand. But that is partly remedied by taking III. iv. as the opening (admittedly very early) of the third day, and not, as is usually done, as the last scene of the second day. (There seems no reason to suppose that the Pages' entry is necessarily on their return from Ford's dinner.) On this basis we have three days, Act I.; II. and III. i.-iii.; and III. iv. to the end. There are still confusions left,[1] but they hardly disconcert the reader, and the producer has to make such adjustments as he sees fit to secure the illusion of stage time which, after all, is all that Shakespeare ever troubled himself about.

Criticism. *Hazlitt.*[2]—*The Merry Wives of Windsor* is no doubt a very amusing play, with a great deal of humour, character, and nature in it: but we should have liked it much better, if any one else had been the hero of it, instead of Falstaff. We could have been contented if Shakespear had not been ' commanded to shew the knight in love.' Wits and philosophers, for the most part, do not shine in that character, and Sir John himself, by no means,

---

[1] *E.g.* ' come to me soon at night ' (II. ii. 259, 279), whereas Ford comes next morning; and Ford's ' yesterday ' in V. i. 14, whereas in fact it was ' this morning.'

[2] *Characters of Shakespear's Plays.*

comes off with flying colours. Many people complain of the degradation and insults to which Don Quixote is so frequently exposed in his various adventures. But what are the unconscious indignities which he suffers, compared with the sensible mortifications which Falstaff is made to bring upon himself? What are the blows and buffetings which the Don receives from the staves of the Yanguesian carriers or from Sancho Panza's more hard-hearted hands, compared with the contamination of the buck-basket, the disguise of the fat woman of Brentford, and the horns of Herne the hunter, which are discovered on Sir John's head? In reading the play we indeed wish him well through all these discomfitures, but it would have been as well if he had not got into them. Falstaff in the *Merry Wives of Windsor* is not the man he was in the two parts of *Henry IV*. His wit and eloquence have left him. Instead of making a butt of others he is made a butt of by them. Neither is there a single particle of love in him to excuse his follies : he is merely a designing barefaced knave, and an unsuccessful one. The scene with Ford as Master Brook, and that with Simple, Slender's man, who comes to ask after the Wise Woman, are almost the only ones in which his old intellectual ascendancy appears. He is like a person recalled to the stage to perform an unaccustomed and ungracious part; and in which we perceive only ' some faint sparks of those flashes of merriment that were wont to set the hearers in a roar.' . . . Nym, Bardolph, and Pistol are but the shadows of what they were; and Justice Shallow himself has little of his consequence left. But his cousin Slender makes up for the deficiency. He is a very potent piece of imbecility. In him the pretensions of the worthy Gloucestershire family are well kept up and immortalised. He and his friend Sackerson and his book of songs and his love of Anne Page and his having nothing to say to her can never be forgotten. It is the only first-rate character in the play: but it is in that class. Shakespear is the only writer who was as great in describing weakness as strength.

Hartley Coleridge.[1]—The Falstaff of the *Merry Wives* is not the Falstaff of *Henry the Fourth*. It is a big-bellied impostor, assuming his name and style, or at best it is Falstaff in dotage. The Mistress Quickly of Windsor is not mine Hostess of the Boar's Head; but she is a very pleasant, busy, good-natured, unprincipled old woman whom it is impossible to be angry with. Shallow should not have left his seat in Gloucestershire and his magisterial duties. Ford's jealousy is of too serious a complexion for the rest of the play. The merry wives are a delightful pair.

Bradley.—Falstaff has been in one respect the most unfortunate of Shakespeare's famous characters. All of them, in passing from the mind of their creator into other minds, suffer change; they tend to lose their harmony through the disproportionate attention bestowed on some one feature, or to lose their uniqueness by being conventionalised into types already familiar. But Falstaff was degraded by Shakespeare himself. The original character is to be found alive in the two parts of *Henry IV*, dead in *Henry V*, and nowhere else. But not very long after these plays were composed, Shakespeare wrote, and he afterwards revised, the very entertaining piece called *The Merry Wives of Windsor*. Perhaps his company wanted a new play on a sudden; or perhaps, as one would rather believe, the tradition may be true that Queen Elizabeth, delighted

[1] *Essays and Marginalia.*

with the Falstaff scenes of *Henry IV*, expressed a wish to see the hero of them again, and to see him in love. Now it was no more possible for Shakespeare to show his own Falstaff in love than to turn twice two into five. But he could write in haste—the tradition says, in a fortnight—a comedy or farce differing from all his other plays in this, that its scene is laid in English middle-class life, and that it is prosaic almost to the end. And among the characters he could introduce a disreputable fat old knight with attendants, and call them Falstaff, Bardolph, Pistol, and Nym. And he could represent this knight assailing, for financial purposes, the virtue of two matrons, and in the event baffled, duped, treated like dirty linen, beaten, burnt, pricked, mocked, insulted, and, worst of all, repentant and didactic. It is horrible. It is almost enough to convince one that Shakespeare himself could sanction the parody of Ophelia in the *Two Noble Kinsmen*. But it no more touches the real Falstaff than Ophelia is degraded by that parody. To picture the real Falstaff befooled like the Falstaff of the *Merry Wives* is like imagining Iago the gull of Roderigo, or Becky Sharp the dupe of Amelia Osborne. Before he had been served the least of these tricks he would have had his brains taken out and buttered, and have given them to a dog for a New Year's gift. I quote the words of the impostor, for after all Shakespeare made him, and gave to him a few sentences worthy of Falstaff himself. But they are only a few—one side of a sheet of notepaper would contain them. And yet critics have solemnly debated at what period in his life Sir John endured the gibes of Master Ford, and whether we should put this comedy between the two parts of *Henry IV*, or between the second of them and *Henry V*. And the Falstaff of the general reader, it is to be feared, is an impossible conglomerate of two distinct characters, while the Falstaff of the mere playgoer is certainly much more like the impostor than the true man.[1]

Unless we bear the gist of these criticisms in mind it is easy to miss much of the pleasure that this play has to give. It is in itself one of the most delightful of all the Shakespearean comedies; it is as lively as all but perhaps one, and more alive than many, since most of the others have a pasteboard or two in the cast, whereas here, with the possible exception of Fenton, there is not a character who is not a human being with the blood flowing in his veins. But we are all too often prevented from throwing ourselves into the spirit of the play by our exasperated bewilderment over Falstaff. And Shakespeare and the Queen between them have not made things any easier for us. If we were watching just a fat disreputable knight being discomfited we could enjoy ourselves. But the Queen did not want just any fat knight; she wanted Falstaff. And so Shakespeare must put the authentic label on the bottle, even though its contents are the poorest moonshine. And he does it all too skilfully, not the less disconcertingly because the impostor speaks most clearly in the true accents exactly at the most inopportune moments, first to Bardolph, and then to Ford after his ducking. The New Cambridge editors would like to excise the un-Falstaffian speeches. I would rather excise those of Bradley's sheet of notepaper, and be free to laugh at a dupe (as one can never laugh at Falstaff) masquerading under an alias to which nothing but a royal command entitles him.

[1] Reprinted from *Oxford Lectures on Poetry* (*The Rejection of Falstaff*) by permission of the Publishers, Macmillan & Co., Ltd.

THE MERRY WIVES OF WINDSOR

DRAMATIS PERSONÆ

SIR JOHN FALSTAFF.

FENTON, *a gentleman.*

SHALLOW, *a country justice.*

SLENDER, *cousin to Shallow.*

FORD, }
PAGE, } *two gentlemen dwelling at Windsor.*

WILLIAM PAGE, *a boy, son to Page.*

SIR HUGH EVANS, *a Welsh parson.*

DOCTOR CAIUS, *a French physician.*

Host of the Garter Inn.

BARDOLPH, }
PISTOL, } *sharpers attending on Falstaff.*
NYM, }

ROBIN, *page to Falstaff.*

SIMPLE, *servant to Slender.*

RUGBY, *servant to Doctor Caius.*

MISTRESS FORD.

MISTRESS PAGE.

ANNE PAGE, *her daughter.*

MISTRESS QUICKLY, *servant to Doctor Caius.*

Servants to Page, Ford, etc.

SCENE: *Windsor, and the neighbourhood.*

THE MERRY WIVES OF WINDSOR

Act First

SCENES I AND II

Windsor.   Before Page's house

Enter Justice Shallow, Slender, and Sir Hugh Evans

Sha. Sir Hugh, persuade me not; I will make a Starchamber matter of it, if he were twenty Sir John
Falstaffs, he shall not abuse Robert Shallow, esquire.

Sle. In the county of Gloucester, justice of peace and
'Coram.'   †

Sha. Ay, cousin Slender, and 'Custalorum.'

Sle. Ay, and 'Ratolorum' too; and a gentleman born,
master parson, who writes himself 'Armigero,'
in any bill, warrant, quittance, or obligation,
'Armigero.'   10

Sha. Ay, that I do, and have done any time these three
hundred years.

Sle. All his successors (gone before him) hath done 't;
and all his ancestors (that come after him) may:
they may give the dozen white luces in their coat.   †

I

Sha. It is an old coat.

Ev. The dozen white louses do become an old coat
well ; it agrees well, passant ; it is a familiar beast †
to man, and signifies love.

Sha. The luce is the fresh fish ; the salt fish is an old coat. †

Sle. I may quarter, coz.   21

Sha. You may, by marrying.

Ev. It is marring indeed, if he quarter it.

Sha. Not a whit.

Ev. Yes, py'r lady ; if he has a quarter of your coat,
there is but three skirts for yourself, in my simple
conjectures : but that is all one.   If Sir John Falstaff
have committed disparagements unto you, I am of
the church, and will be glad to do my benevolence,
to make atonements and compremises between you.   30

Sha. The council shall hear it, it is a riot.

Ev. It is not meet the council hear a riot ; there is no
fear of Got in a riot : the council (look you) shall
desire to hear the fear of Got, and not to hear a
riot ; take your vizaments in that.

Sha. Ha ! o' my life, if I were young again, the sword
should end it.

Ev. It is petter that friends is the sword, and end it : †
and there is also another device in my prain, which
peradventure prings goot discretions with it :—   40

there is Anne Page, which is daughter to Master
Thomas Page, which is pretty virginity.

Sle. Mistress Anne Page? She has brown hair, and
speaks small like a woman.

Ev. It is that fery person for all the 'orld, as just as you
will desire; and seven hundred pounds of moneys,
and gold, and silver, is her grandsire upon his
death's-bed (Got deliver to a joyful resurrections!)
give, when she is able to overtake seventeen years
old: it were a goot motion if we leave our pribbles   50
and prabbles, and desire a marriage between Master
Abraham and Mistress Anne Page.

Sle. Did her grandsire leave her seven hundred pound? †

Ev. Ay, and her father is make her a petter penny.

Sle. I know the young gentlewoman, she has good gifts.

Ev. Seven hundred pounds, and possibilities, is goot
gifts.

Sha. Well, let us see honest Master Page. Is Falstaff
there?

Ev. Shall I tell you a lie? I do despise a liar, as I do   60
despise one that is false, or as I despise one that is
not true. The knight, Sir John, is there; and, I
beseech you, be ruled by your well-willers. I will
peat the door for Master Page. (*Knocks.*) What,
hoa! Got pless your house here!

Pa. (*within*) Who's there?

Enter Page

Ev. Here is Got's plessing and your friend, and Justice
Shallow, and here young Master Slender; that
peradventures shall tell you another tale, if matters
grow to your likings.   70

Pa. I am glad to see your worships well. I thank you
for my venison, Master Shallow.

Sha. Master Page, I am glad to see you: much good do
it your good heart! I wish'd your venison better,
it was ill kill'd. How doth good Mistress Page?—
and I thank you always with my heart, la! with my
heart.

Pa. Sir, I thank you.

Sha. Sir, I thank you; by yea and no, I do.

Pa. I am glad to see you, good Master Slender.   80

Sle. How does your fallow greyhound, sir? I heard say
he was outrun on Cotsall.

Pa. It could not be judg'd, sir.

Sle. You'll not confess, you'll not confess.

Sha. That he will not, 'tis your fault, 'tis your fault; 'tis
a good dog.

Pa. A cur, sir.

Sha. Sir, he's a good dog, and a fair dog, can there be

4

more said ? he is good and fair.   Is Sir John Falstaff
here ?   90

Pa. Sir, he is within ; and I would I could do a good
office between you.

Ev. It is spoke as a Christians ought to speak.

Sha. He hath wrong'd me, Master Page.

Pa. Sir, he doth in some sort confess it.

Sha. If it be confessed, it is not redressed : is not that
so, Master Page ?   He hath wrong'd me, indeed he
hath, at a word : he hath, believe me Robert Shallow,
esquire, saith he is wrong'd.

Pa. Here comes Sir John.   100

Enter Sir John Falstaff, Bardolph, Nym, and Pistol

Fal. Now, Master Shallow, you 'll complain of me to
the king ?

Sha. Knight, you have beaten my men, killed my deer,
and broke open my lodge.

Fal. But not kiss'd your keeper's daughter ?   †

Sha. Tut, a pin ! this shall be answer'd.

Fal. I will answer it straight, I have done all this :
That is now answer'd.

Sha. The council shall know this.

Fal. 'Twere better for you if it were known in counsel : 110
you 'll be laugh'd at.

Ev. *Pauca verba*, Sir John ; goot worts.

Fal. Good worts ? good cabbage. Slender, I broke your
head : what matter have you against me ?

Sle. Marry, sir, I have matter in my head against you,
and against your cony-catching rascals, Bardolph,
Nym, and Pistol. [They carried me to the tavern
and made me drunk, and afterward pick'd my
pocket.]

Bar. You Banbury cheese !   120

Sle. Ay, it is no matter.

Pis. How now, Mephostophilus ?

Sle. Ay, it is no matter.

Nym. Slice, I say ! *pauca, pauca :* slice ! that 's my humour.

Sle. Where 's Simple, my man ? Can you tell, cousin ?

Ev. Peace, I pray you ; now let us understand. There
is three umpires in this matter, as I understand ;
that is, Master Page (fidelicet Master Page), and
there is myself (fidelicet myself), and the three
party is (lastly, and finally) mine host of the Garter. 130

Pa. We three to hear it, and end it between them.

Ev. Fery goot, I will make a prief of it in my note-book ;
and we will afterwards 'ork upon the cause, with
as great discreetly as we can.

Fal. Pistol !

Pis. He hears with ears.

6

Ev. The tevil and his tam! what phrase is this? 'He
    hears with ear'? why, it is affectations.

Fal. Pistol, did you pick Master Slender's purse?

Sle. Ay, by these gloves did he, or I would I might 140
    never come in mine own great chamber again else,
    of seven groats in mill-sixpences, and two Edward
    shovel-boards, that cost me two shilling and two
    pence a-piece of Yead Miller: by these gloves.

Fal. Is this true, Pistol?

Ev. No, it is false, if it is a pick-purse.

Pis. Ha, thou mountain-foreigner! Sir John, and master
      mine,
    I combat challenge of this latten bilbo.
    Word of denial in thy *labras* here!
    Word of denial: froth and scum, thou liest!   150

Sle. By these gloves, then, 'twas he.

Nym. Be avis'd, sir, and pass good humours: I will say
    'marry trap' with you, if you run the nuthook's
    humour on me, that is the very note of it.

Sle. By this hat, then he in the red face had it; for though
    I cannot remember what I did when you made me
    drunk, yet I am not altogether an ass.

Fal. What say you, Scarlet, and John?

Bar. Why, sir, for my part, I say the gentleman had drunk
    himself out of his five sentences.   160

Ev. It is his five senses : fie, what the ignorance is !

Bar. And being fap, sir, was (as they say) cashier'd ; and
so conclusions passed the careires.   †

Sle. Ay, you spake in Latin then too ; but 'tis no matter :
I 'll ne'er be drunk whilst I live again, but in honest,
civil, godly company, for this trick : if I be drunk,
I 'll be drunk with those that have the fear of God,
and not with drunken knaves.

Ev. So Got 'udge me, that is a virtuous mind.

Fal. You hear all these matters denied, gentlemen ; you 170
hear it.

*Enter Anne Page, with wine ; Mistress Ford and
Mistress Page, following*

Pa. Nay, daughter, carry the wine in, we 'll drink within.

Exit Anne Page

Sle. O heaven ! this is Mistress Anne Page.

Pa. How now, Mistress Ford ?

Fal. Mistress Ford, by my troth you are very well met :
by your leave, good mistress.

Kisses her

Pa. Wife, bid these gentlemen welcome. Come, we
have a hot venison pasty to dinner : come, gentlemen, I hope we shall drink down all unkindness.

Exeunt all except Shallow, Slender, and Evans

Sle. I had rather than forty shillings I had my Book of †
    Songs and Sonnets here.   181

                Enter Simple

    How now, Simple, where have you been ? I must
    wait on myself, must I ? You have not the Book
    of Riddles about you, have you ?

Sim. Book of Riddles ? why, did you not lend it to Alice
    Shortcake upon All-hallowmas last, a fortnight
    afore Michaelmas ?

Sha. Come coz, come coz, we stay for you : a word
    with you, coz ; marry this, coz : there is as 'twere
    a tender, a kind of tender, made afar off by Sir Hugh 190
    here. Do you understand me ?

Sle. Ay, sir, you shall find me reasonable ; if it be so, I
    shall do that that is reason.

Sha. Nay, but understand me.

Sle. So I do, sir.

Ev. Give ear to his motions ; Master Slender, I will
    description the matter to you, if you be capacity
    of it.

Sle. Nay, I will do as my cousin Shallow says : I pray
    you pardon me, he 's a justice of peace in his country, 200
    simple though I stand here.

Ev. But that is not the question : the question is con-
    cerning your marriage.

Sha. Ay, there 's the point, sir.

Ev. Marry, is it ; the very point of it, to Mistress Anne
Page.

Sle. Why, if it be so, I will marry her upon any reasonable
demands.

Ev. But can you affection the 'oman ? let us command
to know that of your mouth, or of your lips ; for **210**
divers philosophers hold that the lips is parcel of
the mouth.   Therefore precisely, can you carry your
good will to the maid ?

Sha. Cousin Abraham Slender, can you love her ?

Sle. I hope, sir, I will do as it shall become one that
would do reason.

Ev. Nay, Got's lords, and his ladies ! you must speak
possitable, if you can carry-her your desires †
towards her.

Sha. That you must. Will you (upon good dowry) **220**
marry her ?

Sle. I will do a greater thing than that, upon your request,
cousin, in any reason.

Sha. Nay, conceive me, conceive me, sweet coz : what
I do is to pleasure you, coz : can you love the maid ?

Sle. I will marry her, sir, at your request : but if there
be no great love in the beginning, yet heaven may
decrease it upon better acquaintance, when we are

married, and have more occasion to know one
another : I hope upon familiarity will grow more 230
content : but if you say ' Marry her,' I will marry †
her ; that I am freely dissolved, and dissolutely.

Ev. It is a fery discretion-answer ; save the fall is in
the 'ord ' dissolutely ' : the 'ort is, according to
our meaning, ' resolutely ' : his meaning is good.

Sha. Ay, I think my cousin meant well.

Sle. Ay, or else I would I might be hang'd, la !

Sha. Here comes fair Mistress Anne.

Re-enter Anne Page

Would I were young for your sake, Mistress Anne !

An. The dinner is on the table, my father desires your 240
worships' company.

Sha. I will wait on him, fair Mistress Anne.

Ev. Od's plessed-will ! I will not be absence at the grace.

Exeunt Shallow and Evans

An. Will 't please your worship to come in, sir ?

Sle. No, I thank you forsooth, heartily ; I am very well.

An. The dinner attends you, sir.

Sle. I am not a-hungry, I thank you, forsooth. Go,
sirrah, for all you are my man, go wait upon my
cousin Shallow. (*exit Simple.*) A justice of peace
sometime may be beholding to his friend, for a man ; 250
I keep but three men and a boy yet, till my mother

be dead: but what though? yet I live like a poor
gentleman born.

An. I may not go in without your worship: they will
not sit till you come.

Sle. I' faith, I 'll eat nothing; I thank you as much as
though I did.

An. I pray you, sir, walk in.

Sle. I had rather walk here, I thank you. I bruis'd my
shin th' other day with playing at sword and dagger 260
with a master of fence (three veneys for a dish of
stew'd prunes) [and I with my ward defending my
head, he hot my shin,] and, by my troth, I cannot
abide the smell of hot meat since. Why do your
dogs bark so? be there bears i' the town?

An. I think there are, sir, I heard them talk'd of.

Sle. I love the sport well, but I shall as soon quarrel at it,
as any man in England. You are afraid if you see
the bear loose, are you not?

An Ay, indeed, sir. 270

Sle. That 's meat and drink to me, now: I have seen
Sackerson loose, twenty times, and have taken him
by the chain; but, I warrant you, the women have
so cried and shriek'd at it, that it pass'd: but women,
indeed, cannot abide 'em, they are very ill-favour'd
rough things.

Re-enter Page

Pa. Come, gentle Master Slender, come ; we stay for you.

Sle. I 'll eat nothing, I thank you, sir.

Pa. By cock and pie, you shall not choose, sir ! come,
come.   280

Sle. Nay, pray you lead the way.

Pa. Come on, sir.

Sle. Mistress Anne, yourself shall go first.

An. Not I, sir ; pray you keep on.

Sle. Truly, I will not go first ; truly, la ! I will not do
you that wrong.

An. I pray you, sir.

Sle. I 'll rather be unmannerly than troublesome.   You
do yourself wrong, indeed, la !   *Exeunt*

Enter Sir Hugh Evans and Simple

Ev. Go your ways, and ask of Doctor Caius' house which
is the way : and there dwells one Mistress Quickly ;
which is in the manner of his nurse ; or his try nurse ;
or his cook ; or his laundry ; his washer, and his
wringer.

Sim. Well, sir.

13

Ev. Nay, it is petter yet. Give her this letter; for it is a
'oman that altogether's acquaintance with Mistress
Anne Page; and the letter is to desire and require
her to solicit your master's desires, to Mistress Anne   10
Page. I pray you, be gone: I will make an end of
my dinner; there's pippins and cheese to come.

Exeunt

SCENE III

A room in the Garter Inn

Enter Falstaff, Host, Bardolph, Nym, Pistol, and Robin

Fal. Mine host of the Garter!

Ho. What says my bully-rook? speak scholarly, and
wisely.

Fal. Truly, mine host; I must turn away some of my
followers.

Ho. Discard, bully Hercules, cashier; let them wag;
trot, trot.

Fal. I sit at ten pounds a week.

Ho. Thou 'rt an emperor, Cæsar, Keisar, and Pheezar.
I will entertain Bardolph; he shall draw; he shall   10
tap: said I well, bully Hector?

Fal. Do so, good mine host.

Ho. I have spoke ; let him follow. (*to Bardolph*) Let me
    see thee froth and lime : I am at a word ; follow.
                                          Exit

Fal. Bardolph, follow him : a tapster is a good trade :
    an old cloak makes a new jerkin ; a wither'd serving-
    man a fresh tapster. Go, adieu.

Bar It is a life that I have desir'd : I will thrive.

Pis. O base Hungarian wight ! wilt thou the spigot †
    wield ?   *Exit Bardolph*   20

Nym. He was gotten in drink : [his mind is not heroic :
    and there 's the humour of it :] is not the humour
    conceited ?

Fal. I am glad I am so acquit of this tinder-box : his
    thefts were too open ; his filching was like an un-
    skilful singer, he kept not time.

Nym. The good humour is to steal at a minute's rest.   †

Pis. ' Convey,' the wise it call. ' Steal ? ' foh ! a fico for
    the phrase !

Fal. Well, sirs, I am almost out at heels.   30

Pis. Why then let kibes ensue.

Fal. There is no remedy ; I must cony-catch, I must shift.

Pis. Young ravens must have food.

Fal. Which of you know Ford of this town ?

Pis. I ken the wight : he is of substance good.

Fal. My honest lads, I will tell you what I am about—

Pis. Two yards, and more.

Fal. No quips now, Pistol! (Indeed, I am in the waist
two yards about; but I am now about no waste; I
am about thrift) briefly: I do mean to make love   40
to Ford's wife: I spy entertainment in her; she dis-
courses; she carves; she gives the leer of invitation:
I can construe the action of her familiar style, and the
hardest voice of her behaviour (to be English'd
rightly) is, 'I am Sir John Falstaff's.'

Pis. He hath studied her will; and translated her will; †
out of honesty, into English.

Nym. The anchor is deep: will that humour pass?

Fal. Now, the report goes she has all the rule of her
husband's purse: he hath a legend of angels.   †

Pis. As many devils entertain; and 'To her, boy,' say I.   51

Nym. The humour rises; it is good: humour me the
angels.

Fal. I have writ me here a letter to her: and here another
to Page's wife, who even now gave me good eyes
too; examin'd my parts with most judicious œillades;
sometimes the beam of her view gilded my foot,
sometimes my portly belly.

Pis. Then did the sun on dunghill shine.

Nym. I thank thee for that humour.   60

Fal. O, she did so course o'er my exteriors with such a

greedy intention, that the appetite of her eye did
seem to scorch me up like a burning-glass !   Here's
another letter to her : she bears the purse too ; she
is a region in Guiana ; all gold and bounty.   I will
be cheaters to them both, and they shall be ex-
chequers to me ; they shall be my East and West
Indies, and I will trade to them both.   Go, bear
thou this letter to Mistress Page ; and thou this to
Mistress Ford : we will thrive, lads, we will thrive.   70

Pis.   Shall I Sir Pandarus of Troy become,   †
And by my side wear steel ? then Lucifer take all !

*Nym.*I will run no base humour : here, take the humour-
letter : I will keep the haviour of reputation.

Fal. (*to Rob.*) Hold, sirrah, bear you these letters tightly,
Sail like my pinnace to these golden shores.
Rogues, hence, avaunt, vanish like hailstones, go ;
Trudge ; plod away o' the hoof ; seek shelter, pack !
Falstaff will learn the humour of the age,
French thrift, you rogues, myself, and skirted Page.   †
Exeunt Falstaff and Robin

Pis.   Let vultures gripe thy guts ! for gourd and fullam
holds,   81
And high and low beguiles the rich and poor :
Tester I 'll have in pouch when thou shalt lack,
Base Phrygian Turk !

17

Nym. I have operations, [in my head] which be humours of revenge.

Pis. Wilt thou revenge?

Nym. By Welkin, and her star!   †

Pis. With wit, or steel?

Nym. With both the humours, I: 90
 I will discuss the humour of this love to Page.

Pis. And I to Ford shall eke unfold
  How Falstaff (varlet vile)
 His dove will prove, his gold will hold,
  And his soft couch defile.

Nym. My humour shall not cool: I will incense Page to deal with poison; I will possess him with yellows, † for the revolt of mine is dangerous: that is my true humour.

Pis. Thou art the Mars of malecontents; I second thee; 100 troop on.   *Exeunt*

SCENE IV

A room in Doctor Caius's house

Enter Mistress Quickly, Simple, and Rugby

M.Q. What, John Rugby? I pray thee, go to the casement, and see if you can see my master, Master Doctor Caius, coming. If he do, i' faith, and find anybody

in the house, here will be an old abusing of God's
patience, and the king's English.

Rug. I 'll go watch.

M.Q. Go, and we 'll have a posset for 't soon at night, in
faith, at the latter end of a sea-coal fire. *(exit Rugby.)*
An honest, willing, kind fellow, as ever servant shall
come in house withal ; and I warrant you, no tell-   10
tale, nor no breed-bate : his worst fault is, that he is
given to prayer ; he is something peevish that way ;
but nobody but has his fault ; but let that pass.
Peter Simple, you say your name is ?

Sim. Ay ; for fault of a better.

M.Q. And Master Slender 's your master ?

Sim. Ay, forsooth.

M.Q. Does he not wear a great round beard, like a glover's
paring-knife ?

Sim. No, forsooth : he hath but a little whey face ; with †
a little yellow beard,—a cane-colour'd beard.   21

M.Q. A softly-sprighted man, is he not ?

Sim. Ay, forsooth : but he is as tall a man of his hands
as any is between this and his head ; he hath fought
with a warrener.

M.Q. How say you ?—O, I should remember him : does
he not hold up his head, as it were, and strut in his
gait ?

Sim. Yes, indeed, does he.

M.Q. Well, heaven send Anne Page no worse fortune! 30
Tell Master Parson Evans I will do what I can for
your master: Anne is a good girl, and I wish—

Re-enter Rugby

Rug. Out, alas! here comes my master.

M.Q. We shall all be shent. Run in here, good young
man; go into this closet: he will not stay long.
(Shuts Simple in the closet.) What, John Rugby!
John! what, John, I say! Go, John, go inquire for
my master, I doubt he be not well, that he comes
not home.

(singing) And down, down, adown-a, etc. 40

Enter Doctor Caius

Cai. Vat is you sing? I do not like des toys. Pray you
go and vetch me in my closet un boitier vert,—a
box, a green-a-box: do intend vat I speak? a green-
a-box.

M.Q. Ay, forsooth, I'll fetch it you. *(aside)* I am glad he
went not in himself: if he had found the young
man, he would have been horn-mad.

Cai. Fe, fe, fe, fe! ma foi, il fait fort chaud. Je m'en
vais à la cour,—la grande affaire.

*M.Q.*Is it this, sir ?   50

Cai. Oui ; mette le au mon pocket : dépêche, quickly.
      Vere is dat knave Rugby ?

*M.Q.*What, John Rugby ! John !

Rug. Here, Sir !

Cai. You are John Rugby, and you are Jack Rugby.
      Come, take-a your rapier, and come after my heel
      to the court.

Rug. 'Tis ready, sir, here in the porch.

Cai. By my trot', I tarry too long. Od's me ! Qu'ai-
      ?oublié ? dere is some simples in my closet, dat I   60
      vill not for the varld I shall leave behind.

*M.Q.*Ay me, he 'll find the young man there, and be mad !

Cai. O diable, diable ! vat is in my closet ? Villany !
      larron !   (*Pulling Simple out.*)   Rugby, my rapier !

*M.Q.*Good master, be content.

Cai. Wherefore shall I be content-a ?

*M.Q.*The young man is an honest man.

Cai. What shall de honest man do in my closet ? dere is
      no honest man dat shall come in my closet.

*M.Q.*I beseech you be not so phlegmatic : hear the truth   70
      of it : he came of an errand to me, from Parson
      Hugh.

Cai. Vell ?

Sim. Ay, forsooth ; to desire her to—

*M.Q.*Peace, I pray you.

Cai. Peace-a-your tongue.   Speak-a-your tale.

Sim. To desire this honest gentlewoman, your maid, to
speak a good word to Mistress Anne Page, for my
master in the way of marriage.

*M.Q.*This is all, indeed, la! but I 'll ne'er put my finger   80
in the fire, and need not.

Cai. Sir Hugh send-a you? Rugby, baille me some
paper.   Tarry you a little-a-while.   *Writes*

M.Q. (aside to Sim.) I am glad he is so quiet: if he had
been throughly mov'd, you should have heard him
so loud and so melancholy.   But notwithstanding,
man, I 'll do you your master what good I can: and
the very yea and the no is, the French doctor, my
master,—I may call him my master, look you, for
I keep his house; and I wash, wring, brew, bake,   90
scour, dress meat and drink, make the beds, and do
all myself,—

Sim. (aside to M.Q.) 'Tis a great charge to come under
one body's hand.

M.Q.(aside to Sim.) Are you avis'd o' that? you shall
find it a great charge: and to be up early and down
late;—but notwithstanding, (to tell you in your
ear; I would have no words of it) my master
himself is in love with Mistress Anne Page: but

notwithstanding that I know Anne's mind, that's 100
neither here nor there.

Cai. You, jack'nape ; give-a this letter to Sir Hugh ; by
gar, it is a shallenge : I will cut his troat in de park, †
and I will teach a scurvy jack-a-nape priest to meddle,
or make :—you may be gone ; it is not good you
tarry here.—By gar, I will cut all his two stones ;
by gar, he shall not have a stone to throw at his
dog.   *Exit Simple*

M.Q. Alas, he speaks but for his friend.

Cai. It is no matter-a ver dat :—do not you tell-a-me 110
dat I shall have Anne Page for myself ? By gar,
I vill kill de Jack priest ; and I have appointed
mine host of de Jarteer to measure our weapon.—
By gar, I will myself have Anne Page.

M.Q. Sir, the maid loves you, and all shall be well : we
must give folks leave to prate : what, the good-jer !

Cai. Rugby, come to the court with me.   By gar, if I have
not Anne Page, I shall turn your head out of my door.
Follow my heels, Rugby.   *Exeunt Caius and Rugby*

M.Q. You shall have An fool's-head of your own. No, †
I know Anne's mind for that : never a woman in 121
Windsor knows more of Anne's mind than I do,
nor can do more than I do with her, I thank heaven.

Fen. (*within*) Who's within there, ho ?

M.Q. Who's there, I trow? Come near the house, I, pray you.

Enter Fenton

Fen. How now, good woman, how dost thou?

M.Q. The better that it pleases your good worship to ask.

Fen. What news? how does pretty Mistress Anne?

M.Q. In truth, sir, and she is pretty, and honest, and 130
gentle, and one that is your friend, I can tell you
that by the way; I praise heaven for it.

Fen. Shall I do any good, think'st thou? Shall I not
lose my suit?

M.Q. Troth, sir, all is in his hands above: but notwithstanding, Master Fenton, I'll be sworn on a book
she loves you. Have not your worship a wart
above your eye?

Fen. Yes marry have I, what of that?

M.Q. Well, thereby hangs a tale;—good faith, it is such 140
another Nan; but, I detest, an honest maid as ever
broke bread:—we had an hour's talk of that wart.
—I shall never laugh but in that maid's company!
—But, indeed, she is given too much to allicholy
and musing: but for you—well, go to.

Fen. Well, I shall see her to-day: hold, there's money
for thee; let me have thy voice in my behalf: if
thou seest her before me, commend me.

*M.Q.*Will I ? i' faith, that we will ; and I will tell your
    worship more of the wart the next time we have 150
    confidence, and of other wooers.

Fen. Well, farewell, I am in great haste now.

*M.Q.*Farewell to your worship. (*exit Fenton.*) Truly, an
    honest gentleman : but Anne loves him not ; for
    I know Anne's mind as well as another does.—
    Out upon 't ! what have I forgot ?   *Exit*

Act Second

SCENE I

Before Page's house

Enter Mistress Page, with a letter

*M.P.*What, have I scap'd love-letters in the holiday-
    time of my beauty, and am I now a subject for
    them ? Let me see.   *Reads*
    ' Ask me no reason why I love you, for though
    Love use Reason for his precisian, he admits him †
    not for his counsellor : you are not young, no
    more am I ; go to then, there 's sympathy : you are
    merry, so am I ; ha, ha ! then there 's more sym-

pathy : you love sack, and so do I ; would you
desire better sympathy ? Let it suffice thee, Mistress 10
Page,—at the least if the love of soldier can suffice,
—that I love thee : I will not say, pity me,—'tis
not a soldier-like phrase ; but I say, love me. By
me,

> Thine own true knight,
> By day or night :
> Or any kind of light,
> With all his might,
> For thee to fight.—JOHN FALSTAFF.'

What a Herod of Jewry is this ! O wicked, wicked 20
world ! One that is well-nigh worn to pieces with
age to show himself a young gallant ! What an
unweigh'd behaviour hath this Flemish drunkard
pick'd—with the devil's name !—out of my conversation, that he dares in this manner assay me ?
Why, he hath not been thrice in my company !
What should I say to him ? I was then frugal of
my mirth : Heaven forgive me ! Why, I'll exhibit
a bill in the parliament for the putting down of men.
How shall I be reveng'd on him ? for reveng'd I 30
will be, as sure as his guts are made of puddings.

Enter Mistress Ford

M.F.Mistress Page, trust me, I was going to your house.

*M.P.*And trust me, I was coming to you : you look very
   ill.

*M.F.*Nay, I 'll ne'er believe that ; I have to show to the
   contrary.

*M.P.*Faith, but you do, in my mind.

*M.F.*Well, I do then ; yet, I say, I could show you to
   the contrary. O Mistress Page, give me some
   counsel !   40

*M.P.*What 's the matter, woman ?

*M.F.*O woman, if it were not for one trifling respect, I
   could come to such honour !

*M.P.*Hang the trifle, woman, take the honour.   What is
   it ?—dispense with trifles ;—what is it ?

*M.F.*If I would but go to hell for an eternal moment or
   so, I could be knighted.

*M.P.*What ?   thou liest !   Sir Alice Ford ?   These
   knights will hack, and so thou shouldst not alter
   the article of thy gentry.   50

*M.F.*We burn daylight :—here, read, read ; perceive
   how I might be knighted, I shall think the worse of
   fat men, as long as I have an eye to make difference
   of men's liking : and yet he would not swear ;
   prais'd women's modesty ; and gave such orderly
   and well-behav'd reproof to all uncomeliness, that
   I would have sworn his disposition would have

27

gone to the truth of his words; but they do no
more adhere and keep place together than the
Hundredth Psalm to the tune of 'Green Sleeves.'   60
What tempest, I trow, threw this whale (with so
many tuns of oil in his belly) ashore at Windsor?
How shall I be reveng'd on him? I think the
best way were to entertain him with hope, till the
wicked fire of lust have melted him in his own
grease. Did you ever hear the like?

M.P. Letter for letter, but that the name of Page and
Ford differs: to thy great comfort in this mystery
of ill opinions, here's the twin-brother of thy letter:
but let thine inherit first, for I protest mine never   70
shall. I warrant he hath a thousand of these letters,
writ with blank space for different names,—sure,
more,—and these are of the second edition: he will
print them, out of doubt; for he cares not what he
puts into the press, when he would put us two. I
had rather be a giantess, and lie under Mount
Pelion. Well; I will find you twenty lascivious
turtles ere one chaste man.

M.F. Why, this is the very same; the very hand; the
very words. What doth he think of us?   80

M.P. Nay, I know not: it makes me almost ready to
wrangle with mine own honesty. I'll entertain

myself like one that I am not acquainted withal; for, sure, unless he know some strain in me, that I know not myself, he would never have boarded me in this fury.

M.F.'Boarding,' call you it? I'll be sure to keep him above deck.

*M.P.*So will I: if he come under my hatches, I'll never to sea again. Let's be reveng'd on him: let's   90 appoint him a meeting; give him a show of comfort in his suit, and lead him on with a fine-baited delay, till he hath pawn'd his horses to mine host of the Garter.

*M.F.*Nay, I will consent to act any villany against him, that may not sully the chariness of our honesty. O, that my husband saw this letter! it would give eternal food to his jealousy.

*M.P.*Why, look where he comes; and my good man too: he's as far from jealousy as I am from giving him   100 cause; and that, I hope, is an unmeasurable distance.

*M.F.*You are the happier woman.

*M.P.*Let's consult together against this greasy knight. Come hither.   *They retire*

Enter Ford, with Pistol, and Page, with Nym

Fo. Well, I hope it be not so.

Pis. Hope is a curtal dog in some affairs :
   Sir John affects thy wife.

Fo. Why, sir, my wife is not young.

Pis. He woos both high and low, both rich and poor,
   Both young and old, one with another, Ford ;   110
   He loves the gallimaufry : Ford, perpend.

Fo. Love my wife ?

Pis. With liver burning hot.   Prevent, or go thou,
   Like Sir Actæon he, with Ringwood at thy heels :   †
   O, odious is the name !

Fo. What name, sir ?

Pis. The horn, I say.   Farewell.
   Take heed, have open eye, for thieves do foot by
      night :
   Take heed, ere summer comes, or cuckoo-birds do sing.
   Away sir ; Corporal Nym !—   †
   Believe it, Page, he speaks sense.   *Exit* 121

Fo. (*aside*) I will be patient : I will find out this.

Nym.(*to Page*) And this is true ; I like not the humour
   of lying.   He hath wronged me in some humours :
   I should have borne the humour'd letter to her ; but
   I have a sword, and it shall bite upon my necessity.
   He loves your wife ; there 's the short and the long.
   My name is Corporal Nym ; I speak, and I avouch ;
   'tis true : my name is Nym ; and Falstaff loves your

30

wife.   Adieu.   I love not the humour of bread and 130
cheese; [and there's the humour of it.]   Adieu.   *Exit*

Pa. 'The humour of it,' quoth 'a? here's a fellow
frights English out of his wits.

Fo. I will seek out Falstaff.

Pa. I never heard such a drawling, affecting rogue.

Fo. If I do find it :—well.

Pa. I will not believe such a Cataian, though the priest
o' the town commended him for a true man.

Fo. 'Twas a good sensible fellow :—well.

Pa. How now, Meg !   140

Mrs Page and Mrs Ford come forward

M.P. Whither go you, George ?   Hark you.

M.F. How now, sweet Frank, why art thou melancholy ?

Fo. I melancholy ?   I am not melancholy.   Get you
home, go.

M.F. Faith, thou hast some crotchets in thy head, now :
will you go, Mistress Page ?

M.P. Have with you.   You'll come to dinner, George ?
(*aside to Mrs Ford*) Look who comes yonder : she
shall be our messenger to this paltry knight.

M.F. (*aside to Mrs Page*) Trust me, I thought on her : 150
she'll fit it.

Enter Mistress Quickly

M.P. You are come to see my daughter Anne ?

M.Q. Ay, forsooth ; and, I pray, how does good Mistress
Anne ?

M.P. Go in with us and see : we have an hour's talk with
you.

Exeunt Mrs Page, Mrs Ford, and Mrs Quickly

Pa. How now, Master Ford ?

Fo. You heard what this knave told me, did you not ?

Pa. Yes, and you heard what the other told me ?

Fo. Do you think there is truth in them ?   160

Pa. Hang 'em, slaves !   I do not think the knight would
offer it : but these that accuse him in his intent
towards our wives are a yoke of his discarded men ;
very rogues, now they be out of service.

Fo. Were they his men ?

Pa. Marry were they.

Fo. I like it never the better for that.   Does he lie at the
Garter ?

Pa. Ay marry does he.   If he should intend this voyage
towards my wife, I would turn her loose to him ;   170
and what he gets more of her than sharp words, let
it lie on my head.

Fo. I do not misdoubt my wife ; but I would be loath
to turn them together : a man may be too confident :
I would have nothing lie on my head : I cannot be
thus satisfied.

Pa. Look where my ranting host of the Garter comes :
there is either liquor in his pate, or money in his
purse, when he looks so merrily.

Enter Host

How now, mine host ?   180

Ho. How now, bully-rook ! thou 'rt a gentleman. Cavaleiro-justice, I say !

Enter Shallow

Sha. I follow, mine host, I follow. Good even, and
twenty, good Master Page !   Master Page, will you
go with us ? we have sport in hand.

Ho. Tell him, cavaleiro-justice ; tell him, bully-rook.

Sha. Sir, there is a fray to be fought, between Sir Hugh
the Welsh priest, and Caius the French doctor.

Fo. Good mine host o' the Garter, a word with you.

Drawing him aside

Ho. What say'st thou, my bully-rook ?   190

Sha. (*to Page*) Will you go with us to behold it ?
My merry host hath had the measuring of their
weapons ; and, I think, hath appointed them contrary places ; for, believe me, I hear the parson is
no jester. Hark, I will tell you what our sport
shall be.   *They converse apart*

Ho. Hast thou no suit against my knight, my guest-
cavaleire ?

Fo. None, I protest : but I 'll give you a pottle of
burnt sack to give me recourse to him, and tell him 200
my name is Brook ; only for a jest.

Ho. My hand, bully ; thou shalt have egress and regress,
(said I well ?) and thy name shall be Brook. It is
a merry knight. Will you go, An-heires ? †

Sha. Have with you, mine host.

Pa. I have heard the Frenchman hath good skill in his
rapier.

Sha. Tut, sir, I could have told you more. In these
times you stand on distance ; your passes, stoccadoes, and I know not what : 'tis the heart, Master 210
Page, 'tis here, 'tis here : I have seen the time, with
my long sword, I would have made you four tall
fellows skip like rats.

Ho. Here, boys, here, here ! shall we wag ?

Pa. Have with you : I had rather hear them scold than
fight.   *Exeunt Host, Shallow, and Page*

Fo. Though Page be a secure fool, and stands so firmly
on his wife's frailty, yet I cannot put off my opinion
so easily : she was in his company at Page's house ;
and what they made there, I know not. Well, I will 220
look further into 't, and I have a disguise, to sound
Falstaff ; if I find her honest, I lose not my labour ;
if she be otherwise, 'tis labour well bestow'd.   *Exit*

SCENE II

A room in the Garter Inn

Enter Falstaff and Pistol

[*Pis.* I will retort the sum in equipage.]

Fal. I will not lend thee a penny.

Pis. Why then the world 's mine oyster,
Which I with sword will open.

Fal. Not a penny.   I have been content, sir, you should
lay my countenance to pawn : I have grated upon
my good friends for three reprieves for you, and your
coach-fellow Nym ; or else you had looked through
the grate, like a geminy of baboons.   I am damn'd
in hell, for swearing to gentlemen my friends, you   10
were good soldiers, and tall fellows ; and when
Mistress Bridget lost the handle of her fan, I took 't
upon mine honour thou hadst it not.

Pis. Didst not thou share ? hadst thou not fifteen pence ?

Fal. Reason, you rogue, reason : think'st thou I 'll
endanger my soul gratis ?   At a word, hang no
more about me, I am no gibbet for you.   Go—a
short knife and a throng !—to your manor of Pickt-
hatch !   Go ; you 'll not bear a letter for me, you
rogue ? you stand upon your honour ?   Why, thou   20

unconfinable baseness, it is as much as I can do to
keep the terms of my honour precise: I, I, I myself
sometimes, leaving the fear of God on the left hand,
and hiding mine honour in my necessity, am fain to
shuffle, to hedge, and to lurch; and yet you, you †
rogue, will ensconce your rags, your cat-a-mountain
looks, your red-lattice phrases, and your bold-beating
oaths, under the shelter of your honour! You will
not do it? you?

Pis. I do relent: what would thou more of man?   30

Enter Robin

Rob. Sir, here's a woman would speak with you.
Fal. Let her approach.

Enter Mistress Quickly

M.Q. Give your worship good morrow.
Fal. Good morrow, good wife.
M.Q. Not so, an't please your worship.
Fal. Good maid, then.
M.Q. I'll be sworn,
　　As my mother was, the first hour I was born.
Fal. I do believe the swearer. What with me?
M.Q. Shall I vouchsafe your worship a word or two?   40
Fal. Two thousand, fair woman: an I'll vouchsafe thee
　　the hearing.

M.Q. There is one Mistress Ford, sir :—I pray, come a
little nearer this ways :—I myself dwell with Master
Doctor Caius,—

Fal. Well, on : Mistress Ford, you say,—

M.Q. Your worship says very true :—I pray your worship,
come a little nearer this ways.

Fal. I warrant thee, nobody hears ;—mine own people,
mine own people.   50

M.Q. Are they so ?   God bless them, and make them
his servants !

Fal. Well ; Mistress Ford, what of her ?

M.Q. Why, sir, she 's a good creature.—Lord, Lord !
your worship 's a wanton !   Well, heaven forgive
you, and all of us, I pray !

Fal. Mistress Ford ;—come, Mistress Ford,—

M.Q. Marry, this is the short and the long of it ; you
have brought her into such a canaries, as 'tis wonderful.   The best courtier of them all, when the court   60
lay at Windsor, could never have brought her to
such a canary.   Yet there has been knights, and
lords, and gentlemen, with their coaches ; I warrant
you, coach after coach, letter after letter, gift after
gift, smelling so sweetly ; all musk, and so rushling,
I warrant you, in silk and gold, and in such alligant
terms, and in such wine and sugar of the best, and

the fairest, that would have won any woman's heart ;
and, I warrant you, they could never get an eye-wink
of her : I had myself twenty angels given me this 70
morning, but I defy all angels (in any such sort, as
they say) but in the way of honesty : and, I warrant
you, they could never get her so much as sip on a
cup with the proudest of them all, and yet there has
been earls ; nay (which is more) pensioners ; but,
I warrant you, all is one with her.

Fal. But what says she to me ? be brief, my good she-
Mercury.

M.Q. Marry, she hath receiv'd your letter ; for the which
she thanks you a thousand times ; and she gives 80
you to notify, that her husband will be absence
from his house, between ten and eleven.

Fal. Ten, and eleven.

M.Q. Ay, forsooth ; and then you may come and see
the picture, she says, that you wot of : Master Ford,
her husband, will be from home. Alas, the sweet
woman leads an ill life with him ! he 's a very jealousy
man : she leads a very frampold life with him, good
heart.

Fal. Ten, and eleven. Woman, commend me to her, I 90
will not fail her.

M.Q. Why, you say well. But I have another messenger

to your worship.   Mistress Page hath her hearty
commendations to you too : and let me tell you in
your ear, she 's as fartuous a civil modest wife, and
one, I tell you, that will not miss you morning nor
evening prayer, as any is in Windsor, whoe'er be the
other : and she bade me tell your worship that her
husband is seldom from home ; but she hopes there
will come a time.   I never knew a woman so dote 100
upon a man : surely, I think you have charms, la ;
yes, in truth.

Fal. Not I, I assure thee : setting the attraction of my
good parts aside, I have no other charms.

M.Q. Blessing on your heart for 't !

Fal. But I pray thee tell me this : has Ford's wife and
Page's wife acquainted each other how they love
me ?

M.Q. That were a jest indeed ! they have not so little grace,
I hope : that were a trick indeed !   But Mistress 110
Page would desire you to send her your little page,
of all loves : her husband has a marvellous infection
to the little page ; and, truly, Master Page is an
honest man.   Never a wife in Windsor leads a better
life than she does : do what she will, say what she
will, take all, pay all, go to bed when she list, rise
when she list, all is as she will : and truly she deserves

it ; for if there be a kind woman in Windsor, she is
one. You must send her your page, no remedy.

Fal. Why, I will. 120

*M.Q.*Nay, but do so, then, and look you, he may come
and go between you both ; and in any case have a
nay-word, that you may know one another's mind,
and the boy never need to understand any thing ;
for 'tis not good that children should know any
wickedness : old folks, you know, have discretion,
as they say, and know the world.

Fal. Fare thee well, commend me to them both : there 's
my purse, I am yet thy debtor. Boy, go along with
this woman. (*exeunt Mistress Quickly and Robin.*) 130
This news distracts me !

Pis. This punk is one of Cupid's carriers : †
Clap on more sails, pursue ; up with your fights :
Give fire : she is my prize, or ocean whelm them all !
Exit

Fal. Say'st thou so ? Old Jack, go thy ways ; I 'll make
more of thy old body than I have done. Will they
yet look after thee ? Wilt thou, after the expense
of so much money, be now a gainer ? Good body,
I thank thee. Let them say 'tis grossly done, so it
be fairly done, no matter. 140

Enter Bardolph

Bar. Sir John, there's one Master Brook below would
fain speak with you, and be acquainted with you;
and hath sent your worship a morning's draught of
sack.

Fal. Brook is his name?

Bar. Ay, sir.

Fal. Call him in. (*exit Bardolph.*) Such Brooks are welcome to me, that o'erflows such liquor. Ah, ha!
Mistress Ford and Mistress Page, have I encompass'd
you? go to; *via!*   150

Re-enter Bardolph, with Ford disguised

Fo. Bless you, sir!

Fal. And you, sir! Would you speak with me?

Fo. I make bold, to press with so little preparation upon
you.

Fal. You're welcome. What's your will?—Give us
leave, drawer.   *Exit Bardolph*

Fo. Sir, I am a gentleman that have spent much; my
name is Brook.

Fal. Good Master Brook, I desire more acquaintance of
you.   160

Fo. Good Sir John, I sue for yours: not to charge you;
for I must let you understand I think myself in
better plight for a lender than you are: the which

41

    hath something embolden'd me to this unseason'd
    intrusion ; for they say, if money go before, all
    ways do lie open.

Fal. Money is a good soldier, sir, and will on.

Fo. Troth, and I have a bag of money here troubles me :
    if you will help to bear it, Sir John, take all, or half,
    for easing me of the carriage. 170

Fal. Sir, I know not how I may deserve to be your porter.

Fo. I will tell you, sir, if you will give me the hearing.

Fal. Speak, good Master Brook : I shall be glad to be
    your servant.

Fo. Sir, I hear you are a scholar, (I will be brief with
    you) and you have been a man long known to me,
    though I had never so good means, as desire, to make
    myself acquainted with you.   I shall discover a thing
    to you, wherein I must very much lay open mine
    own imperfection : but, good Sir John, as you 180
    have one eye upon my follies, as you hear them un-
    folded, turn another into the register of your own,
    that I may pass with a reproof the easier, sith you
    yourself know how easy it is to be such an offender.

Fal. Very well, sir ; proceed.

Fo. There is a gentlewoman in this town, her husband's
    name is Ford.

Fal. Well, sir.

Fo. I have long lov'd her, and, I protest to you, bestowed
   much on her ; followed her with a doting observ-   190
   ance ; engross'd opportunities to meet her ; fee'd
   every slight occasion that could but niggardly give
   me sight of her ; not only bought many presents to
   give her, but have given largely to many, to know
   what she would have given ; briefly, I have pursued
   her, as love hath pursued me, which hath been on
   the wing of all occasions.   But whatsoever I have
   merited, either in my mind, or in my means, meed
   I am sure I have received none, unless experience
   be a jewel that I have purchased at an infinite rate,   200
   and that hath taught me to say this :
   ' Love like a shadow flies, when substance love
       pursues,
   Pursuing that that flies, and flying what pursues.'

Fal. Have you receiv'd no promise of satisfaction at her
   hands ?

Fo. Never.

Fal. Have you importun'd her to such a purpose ?

Fo. Never.

Fal. Of what quality was your love, then ?

Fo. Like a fair house, built on another man's ground,   210
   so that I have lost my edifice, by mistaking the place
   where I erected it.

Fal. To what purpose have you unfolded this to me?

Fo. When I have told you that, I have told you all.
Some say, that though she appear honest to me,
yet in other places she enlargeth her mirth so far that
there is shrewd construction made of her. Now,
Sir John, here is the heart of my purpose: you are
a gentleman of excellent breeding, admirable dis-
course, of great admittance, authentic in your place 220
and person, generally allow'd for your many war-
like, court-like, and learned preparations.

Fal. O, sir!

Fo. Believe it, for you know it. There is money;
spend it, spend it, spend more; spend all I have,
only give me so much of your time in exchange of
it, as to lay an amiable siege to the honesty of this
Ford's wife: use your art of wooing; win her to
consent to you: if any man may, you may as soon
as any. 230

Fal. Would it apply well to the vehemency of your
affection, that I should win what you would enjoy? Methinks you prescribe to yourself very pre-
posterously.

Fo. O, understand my drift. She dwells so securely
on the excellency of her honour, that the folly of
my soul dares not present itself: she is too bright

to be look'd against. Now, could I come to her
with any detection in my hand, my desires had
instance and argument to commend themselves : I 240
could drive her then from the ward of her purity,
her reputation, her marriage-vow, and a thousand
other her defences, which now are too too strongly
embattled against me. What say you to 't, Sir
John ?

Fal. Master Brook, I will first make bold with your
money ; next, give me your hand ; and last, as I
am a gentleman, you shall, if you will, enjoy Ford's
wife.

Fo. O good sir ! 250

Fal. I say you shall.

Fo. Want no money, Sir John, you shall want none.

Fal. Want no Mistress Ford, Master Brook, you shall
want none. I shall be with her (I may tell you) by
her own appointment ; even as you came in to me,
her assistant, or go-between, parted from me : I
say I shall be with her between ten and eleven ; for
at that time the jealous rascally knave her husband
will be forth. Come you to me at night, you shall
know how I speed. 260

Fo. I am blest in your acquaintance. Do you know
Ford, sir ?

45

Fal. Hang him, poor cuckoldly knave, I know him not :
yet I wrong him to call him poor ; they say the
jealous wittolly knave hath masses of money, for †
the which his wife seems to me well-favour'd : I will
use her as the key of the cuckoldly rogue's coffer,
and there 's my harvest-home.

Fo. I would you knew Ford, sir, that you might avoid
him, if you saw him.   270

Fal. Hang him, mechanical salt-butter rogue ; I will
stare him out of his wits ; I will awe him with my
cudgel : it shall hang like a meteor o'er the cuckold's
horns.   Master Brook, thou shalt know I will pre-
dominate over the peasant, and thou shalt lie with
his wife.   Come to me soon at night.   Ford 's a
knave, and I will aggravate his style ; thou, Master
Brook, shalt know him for knave, and cuckold.
Come to me soon at night.   *Exit*

Fo. What a damn'd Epicurean rascal is this ! My   280
heart is ready to crack with impatience.   Who says
this is improvident jealousy ? my wife hath sent
to him, the hour is fix'd, the match is made : would
any man have thought this ?   See the hell of having
a false woman !   My bed shall be abus'd, my coffers
ransack'd, my reputation gnawn at, and I shall not
only receive this villanous wrong, but stand under

the adoption of abominable terms, and by him that does me this wrong.   Terms ! names !—Amaimon sounds well ; Lucifer, well ; Barbason, well ; yet 290 they are devils' additions, the names of fiends : but Cuckold, Wittol, Cuckold ? the devil himself hath not such a name.   Page is an ass, a secure ass : he will trust his wife ; he will not be jealous.   I will rather trust a Fleming with my butter, Parson Hugh the Welshman with my cheese, an Irishman with my aqua-vitæ bottle, or a thief to walk my ambling gelding, than my wife with herself : then she plots, then she ruminates, then she devises ; and what they think in their hearts they may effect, they will break 300 their hearts but they will effect.   God be prais'd for my jealousy !—Eleven o'clock the hour.   I will prevent this, detect my wife, be reveng'd on Falstaff, and laugh at Page.   I will about it, better three hours too soon, than a minute too late.   Fie, fie, fie ! cuckold ! cuckold ! cuckold !   *Exit*

SCENE III

A field near Windsor

Enter Caius and Rugby

Cai. Jack Rugby!

Rug. Sir?

Cai. Vat is de clock, Jack?

Rug. 'Tis past the hour, sir, that Sir Hugh promis'd to meet.

Cai. By gar, he has save his soul, dat he is no-come; he has pray his Pible well, dat he is no-come: by gar, Jack Rugby, he is dead already, if he be come.

Rug. He is wise, sir; he knew your worship would kill him if he came.   10

Cai. By gar, de herring is no dead, so as I vill kill him. Take your rapier, Jack, I vill tell you how I vill kill him.

Rug. Alas, sir, I cannot fence.

Cai. Villainy, take your rapier.

Rug. Forbear; here's company.

Enter Host, Shallow, Slender, and Page

Ho. Bless thee, bully doctor!

Sha. Save you, Master Doctor Caius!

Pa. Now, good master doctor !

Sle. Give you good morrow, sir.   20

Cai. Vat be all you, one, two, tree, four, come for ?

Ho. To see thee fight, to see thee foin, to see thee traverse,
to see thee here, to see thee there, to see thee pass
thy punto, thy stock, thy reverse, thy distance, thy †
montant.   Is he dead, my Ethiopian ? is he dead,
my Francisco ? ha, bully !   What says my Æsculapius ? my Galen ? my heart of elder ? ha ! is he
dead, bully-stale ? is he dead ?   †

Cai. By gar, he is de coward Jack priest of de vorld ; he
is not show his face.   30

Ho. Thou art a Castalion-King-Urinal.   Hector of
Greece, my boy !

Cai. I pray you, bear vitness that me have stay, six or
seven, two tree hours for him, and he is no-come.

Sha. He is the wiser man, master doctor : he is a curer
of souls, and you a curer of bodies ; if you should
fight, you go against the hair of your professions.
Is it not true, Master Page ?

Pa. Master Shallow, you have yourself been a great
fighter, though now a man of peace.   40

Sha. Bodykins, Master Page, though I now be old, and
of the peace, if I see a sword out, my finger itches to
make one.   Though we are justices, and doctors, and

churchmen, Master Page, we have some salt of our
youth in us, we are the sons of women, Master
Page.

Pa. 'Tis true, Master Shallow.

Sha. It will be found so, Master Page. Master Doctor
Caius, I am come to fetch you home. I am sworn
of the peace: you have shew'd yourself a wise   50
physician, and Sir Hugh hath shewn himself a wise
and patient churchman. You must go with me,
master doctor.

Ho. Pardon, guest-justice.—A [word,] Mounseur Mock- †
water.

Cai. Mock-vater? vat is dat?

Ho. Mock-water, in our English tongue, is valour, bully.

Cai. By gar, den, I have as much mock-vater as de
Englishman.—Scurvy Jack-dog priest! by gar, me
vill cut his ears.   60

Ho. He will clapper-claw thee tightly, bully.

Cai. Clapper-de-claw? vat is dat?

Ho. That is, he will make thee amends.

Cai. By gar, me do look he shall clapper-de-claw me;
for, by gar, me vill have it.

Ho. And I will provoke him to 't, or let him wag.

Cai. Me tank you for dat.

Ho. And, moreover, bully,—But first, master guest, and

Master Page, and eke Cavaleiro Slender, go you
through the town to Frogmore.   *Aside to them*   70
Pa. Sir Hugh is there, is he?
Ho. He is there : see what humour he is in ; and I will
bring the doctor about by the fields. Will it do
well ?
Sha. We will do it.
Pa., Sha., and Sle. Adieu, good master doctor.
                    Exeunt Page, Shallow, and Slender
Cai. By gar, me vill kill de priest, for he speak for a
jack-an-ape to Anne Page.
Ho. Let him die : sheathe thy impatience ; throw cold †
water on thy choler : go about the fields with me   80
through Frogmore, I will bring thee where Mistress
Anne Page is, at a farm-house a-feasting ; and thou
shalt woo her.   Cried-game, said I well ?   †
Cai. By gar, me dank you vor dat : by gar, I love you ;
and I shall procure-a you de good guest ; de earl,
de knight, de lords, de gentlemen, my patients.
Ho. For the which, I will be thy adversary toward Anne
Page.   Said I well ?
Cai. By gar, 'tis good ; vell said.
Ho. Let us wag, then.   90
Cai. Come at my heels, Jack Rugby.   *Exeunt*

Act Third

SCENE I

A field near Frogmore

Enter Sir Hugh Evans and Simple

Ev. I pray you now, good Master Slender's serving-
man, and friend Simple by your name, which way
have you look'd for Master Caius, that calls himself
doctor of physic ?

Sim. Marry, sir, the pittie-ward, the park-ward, every
way ; old Windsor way, and every way but the
town way.

Ev. I most fehemently desire you you will also look that
way.

Sim. I will, sir. *Exit* 10

Ev. Jeshu pless me ! how full of chollors I am, and
trempling of mind ; I shall be glad if he have deceiv'd me ; how melancholies I am !—I will knog
his urinals about his knave's costard when I have
goot opportunities for the 'ork.—Pless my soul !—
Sings

> To shallow rivers, to whose falls   †
> Melodious birds sings madrigals ;
> There will we make our peds of roses,
> And a thousand fragrant posies.
> To shallow—   20

Now, so Kad 'udge me, I have a great dispositions
to cry.   *Sings*

> Melodious birds sing madrigals—
> Whenas I sat in Pabylon—
> And a thousand vagram posies.
> To shallow etc.

Re-enter Simple

Sim. Yonder he is coming, this way, Sir Hugh.

Ev. He 's welcome.—   *Sings*

> To shallow rivers, to whose falls—

Heaven prosper the right !—What weapon is he ?   30

Sim. No weapons, sir.   There comes my master, Master
Shallow, and another gentleman ; from Frogmore,
over the stile, this way.

Ev. Pray you give me my gown, or else keep it in your
arms.

Enter Page, Shallow, and Slender

Sha. How now, master parson ?   Good morrow, good
Sir Hugh.   Keep a gamester from the dice, and a
good student from his book, and it is wonderful.

Sle. (*aside*) Ah, sweet Anne Page !

Pa. God save you, good Sir Hugh ! 40

Ev. Got pless you from his mercy sake, all of you !

Sha. What, the sword, and the word ? do you study them both, master parson ?

Pa. And youthful still, in your doublet and hose, this raw rheumatic day !

Ev. There is reasons, and causes for it.

Pa. We are come to you, to do a good office, master parson.

Ev. Fery well : what is it ?

Pa. Yonder is a most reverend gentleman ; who, belike, 50 having receiv'd wrong by some person, is at most odds with his own gravity and patience that ever you saw.

Sha. I have lived fourscore years, and upward ; I never heard a man of his place, gravity, and learning, so wide of his own respect.

Ev. What is he ?

Pa. I think you know him ; Master Doctor Caius, the renown'd French physician.

Ev. Got's will, and his passion of my heart ! I had **as** 60 lief you would tell me of a mess of porridge.

Pa. Why ?

Ev. He has no more knowledge in Hibocrates and

Galen, and he is a knave besides; a cowardly
knave as you would desires to be acquainted
withal.

Pa. I warrant you, he 's the man should fight with him.

Sle. (*aside*) O sweet Anne Page !

Sha. It appears so by his weapons : keep them asunder :
here comes Doctor Caius.

Enter Host, Caius, and Rugby

Pa. Nay, good master parson, keep in your weapon.   70

Sha. So do you, good master doctor.

Ho. Disarm them, and let them question : let them keep
their limbs whole, and hack our English.

Cai. I pray you let-a me speak a word with your ear.
Verefore vill you not meet-a me ?

Ev. (*aside to Caius*) Pray you, use your patience : in
good time.

Cai. By gar, you are de coward ; de Jack dog ; John
Ape.

Ev. (*aside to Caius*) Pray you let us not be laughing-   80
stocks to other men's humours ; I desire you in
friendship, and I will one way or other make you
amends.   (*aloud*) Py Jeshu, I will knog your
urinal about your knave's cogscomb [for missing
your meetings and appointments].

Cai. Diable !—Jack Rugby,—mine host de Jarteer,— have I not stay for him, to kill him ? have I not at de place I did appoint ?

Ev. As I am a Christians soul, now look you ; this is the place appointed : I 'll be judgement by mine host   90 of the Garter.

Ho. Peace, I say, Gallia and Gaul, French and Welsh, soul-curer and body-curer !

Cai. Ay, dat is very good, excellent.

Ho. Peace, I say ! hear mine host of the Garter. Am I politic ? am I subtle ? am I a Machiavel ? Shall I lose my doctor ? no, he gives me the potions and the motions. Shall I lose my parson ? my priest ? my Sir Hugh ? no, he gives me the proverbs, and the no-verbs. [Give me thy hand, terrestrial ; so.]   100 Give me thy hand, celestial ; so. Boys of art, I have deceiv'd you both ; I have directed you to wrong places ; your hearts are mighty, your skins are whole, and let burnt sack be the issue. Come, lay their swords to pawn. Follow me, lads of peace ; follow, follow, follow.

Sha. Afore God, a mad host. Follow, gentlemen, follow.

Sle. (*aside*) O sweet Anne Page !

Exeunt Shallow, Slender, Page, and Host

Cai. Ha, do I perceive dat ? have you make-a de sot of 11c us, ha, ha ?

Ev. This is well, he has made us his vlouting-stog : I desire you that we may be friends ; and let us knog our prains together to be revenge on this same scall, scurvy, cogging companion, the host of the Garter.

Cai. By gar, with all my heart. He promise to bring me where is Anne Page ; by gar, he deceive me too.

Ev. Well, I will smite his noddles : pray you follow.

Exeunt

SCENE II

The street, in Windsor

Enter Mistress Page and Robin

M.P. Nay, keep your way, little gallant ; you were wont to be a follower, but now you are a leader. Whether had you rather lead mine eyes, or eye your master's heels ?

Rob. I had rather, forsooth, go before you like a man, than follow him like a dwarf.

M.P. O, you are a flattering boy, now I see you 'll be a courtier.

Enter Ford

Fo. Well met, Mistress Page, whither go you ;

M.P. Truly, sir, to see your wife ; is she at home ?   10

Fo. Ay, and as idle as she may hang together, for want
of company. I think, if your husbands were dead,
you two would marry.

M.P. Be sure of that,—two other husbands.

Fo. Where had you this pretty weathercock ?

M.P. I cannot tell what the dickens his name is my husband
had him of.—What do you call your knight's name,
sirrah ?

Rob. Sir John Falstaff.

Fo. Sir John Falstaff ?   20

M.P. He, he, I can never hit on 's name. There is such
a league between my good man and he !—Is your
wife at home indeed ?

Fo. Indeed she is.

M.P. By your leave, sir, I am sick till I see her.

Exeunt Mrs Page and Robin

Fo. Has Page any brains ? hath he any eyes ? hath he
any thinking ?   Sure they sleep, he hath no use of
them. Why, this boy will carry a letter twenty
mile, as easy as a cannon will shoot point-blank
twelve score. He pieces out his wife's inclination ;   30
he gives her folly motion and advantage : and now
she 's going to my wife, and Falstaff's boy with her.
A man may hear this shower sing in the wind. And

58

Falstaff's boy with her !   Good plots, they are laid,
and our revolted wives share damnation together.
Well, I will take him, then torture my wife, pluck
the borrow'd veil of modesty from the so-seeming
Mistress Page, divulge Page himself for a secure and
wilful Actæon, and to these violent proceedings all
my neighbours shall cry aim.   (*Clock heard.*)   The   40
clock gives me my cue, and my assurance bids me
search, there I shall find Falstaff : I shall be rather
prais'd for this than mock'd, for it is as positive as
the earth is firm that Falstaff is there : I will go.

Enter Page, Shallow, Slender, Host, Sir Hugh Evans,
Caius, and Rugby

Sha., Page, &c. Well met, Master Ford.

Fo. Trust me, a good knot : I have good cheer at home,
and I pray you all go with me.

Sha. I must excuse myself, Master Ford.

Sle. And so must I sir, we have appointed to dine with
Mistress Anne, and I would not break with her for   50
more money than I 'll speak of.

Sha. We have linger'd about a match between Anne Page
and my cousin Slender, and this day we shall have
our answer.

Sle. I hope I have your good will, father Page.

Pa. You have, Master Slender, I stand wholly for you, but my wife, master doctor, is for you altogether.

Cai. Ay, be-gar, and de maid is love-a me : my nursh-a Quickly tell me so mush.

Ho. What say you to young Master Fenton ? he capers, 60 he dances, he has eyes of youth ; he writes verses, he speaks holiday, he smells April and May, he will carry 't, he will carry 't, 'tis in his buttons, he will † carry 't.

Pa. Not by my consent, I promise you. The gentleman is of no having, he kept company with the wild prince and Poins ; he is of too high a region ; he knows too much. No, he shall not knit a knot in his fortunes with the finger of my substance : if he take her, let him take her simply ; the wealth I have 70 waits on my consent, and my consent goes not that way.

Fo. I beseech you heartily, some of you go home with me to dinner : besides your cheer, you shall have sport, I will show you a monster. Master doctor, you shall go, so shall you, Master Page, and you, Sir Hugh.

Sha. Well, fare you well : we shall have the freer wooing at Master Page's. *Exeunt Shallow and Slender*

Cai. Go home, John Rugby ; I come anon. *Exit Rugby* 80

Ho. Farewell, my hearts, I will to my honest knight
　　Falstaff, and drink canary with him.　　　*Exit*

Fo. (*aside*) I think I shall drink in pipe-wine first with
　　him, I'll make him dance.　Will you go, gentles?

All. Have with you, to see this monster.　　*Exeunt*

SCENE III

A room in Ford's house

Enter Mistress Ford and Mistress Page

M.F. What, John! What, Robert!

M.P. Quickly, quickly!—is the buck-basket—

M.F. I warrant.　What, Robin, I say!

Enter Servants with a great buck-basket

M.P. Come, come, come.

M.F. Here, set it down.

M.P. Give your men the charge, we must be brief.

M.F. Marry, as I told you before, John and Robert, be
　　ready here hard by in the brew-house, and when I
　　suddenly call you, come forth, and (without any
　　pause, or staggering) take this basket on your　　**10**
　　shoulders: that done, trudge with it in all haste,
　　and carry it among the whitsters in Datchet Mead,

and there empty it in the muddy ditch, close by the
Thames side.

M.P. You will do it?

M.F. I ha' told them over and over, they lack no direction.
Be gone, and come when you are call'd.

Exeunt Servants

M.P. Here comes little Robin.

Enter Robin

M.F. How now, my eyas-musket, what news with you?

Rob. My master, Sir John, is come in at your back-door,   20
Mistress Ford, and requests your company.

M.P. You little Jack-a-Lent, have you been true to us?

Rob. Ay, I'll be sworn.   My master knows not of your
being here; and hath threaten'd to put me into
everlasting liberty, if I tell you of it; for he swears
he'll turn me away.

M.P. Thou'rt a good boy: this secrecy of thine shall be
a tailor to thee, and shall make thee a new doublet
and hose.   I'll go hide me.

M.F. Do so.   Go tell thy master I am alone.   *(exit Robin.)*   30
Mistress Page, remember you your cue.

M.P. I warrant thee, if I do not act it, hiss me.   *Exit*

M.F. Go to, then: we'll use this unwholesome humidity,
this gross watery pumpion; we'll teach him to
know turtles from jays.

Enter Falstaff

Fal. ' Have I caught ' thee, ' my heavenly jewel ? '   Why, †
now let me die, for I have liv'd long enough : this is
the period of my ambition : O this blessed hour !

M.F. O sweet Sir John !

Fal. Mistress Ford, I cannot cog, I cannot prate, Mistress   40
Ford ; now shall I sin in my wish : I would thy
husband were dead, I 'll speak it before the best
lord, I would make thee my lady.

M.F. I your lady, Sir John ?   alas, I should be a pitiful
lady !

Fal. Let the court of France show me such another.   I
see how thine eye would emulate the diamond :
thou hast the right arched beauty of the brow, that
becomes the ship-tire, the tire-valiant, or any tire of
Venetian admittance.   50

M.F. A plain kerchief, Sir John : my brows become
nothing else, nor that well neither.

Fal. By the Lord, thou art a traitor to say so : thou †
wouldst make an absolute courtier, and the firm
fixture of thy foot would give an excellent motion
to thy gait, in a semicircled farthingale.   I see what
thou wert, if Fortune thy foe were not, Nature thy †
friend.   Come, thou canst not hide it.

M.F. Believe me, there 's no such thing in me.

Fal. What made me love thee ? Let that persuade thee : 60
there's something extraordinary in thee : come, I
cannot cog, and say thou art this and that, like a
many of these lisping hawthorn-buds, that come
like women in men's apparel, and smell like Bucklers- †
bury in simple time ; I cannot, but I love thee, none
but thee ; and thou deserv'st it.

M.F. Do not betray me, sir, I fear you love Mistress Page.

Fal. Thou mightst as well say, I love to walk by the
Counter-gate, which is as hateful to me as the reek †
of a lime-kiln. 70

M.F. Well, heaven knows how I love you, and you shall
one day find it.

Fal. Keep in that mind, I 'll deserve it.

M.F. Nay, I must tell you, so you do ; or else I could not
be in that mind.

Rob. (*within*) Mistress Ford, Mistress Ford ! here 's Mistress
Page at the door, sweating, and blowing, and looking
wildly, and would needs speak with you presently.

Fal. She shall not see me, I will ensconce me behind the
arras. 80

M.F. Pray you do so, she 's a very tattling woman.

Falstaff hides himself
Re-enter Mistress Page and Robin

What 's the matter ? how now ?

*M.P.*O Mistress Ford, what have you done? You're sham'd, you're overthrown, you're undone for ever!

*M.F.*What's the matter, good Mistress Page?

*M.P.*O well-a-day, Mistress Ford! having an honest man to your husband, to give him such cause of suspicion!

*M.F.*What cause of suspicion?   90

*M.P.*What cause of suspicion? Out upon you! how am I mistook in you!

*M.F.*Why, alas, what's the matter?

*M.P.*Your husband's coming hither, woman, with all the officers in Windsor, to search for a gentleman, that he says is here now in the house; by your consent to take an ill advantage of his absence: you are undone.

M.F.'Tis not so, I hope.

*M.P.*Pray heaven it be not so, that you have such a man 100 here! but 'tis most certain your husband's coming, with half Windsor at his heels, to search for such a one; I come before to tell you. If you know yourself clear, why, I am glad of it; but if you have a friend here, convey, convey him out. Be not amaz'd, call all your senses to you, defend your reputation, or bid farewell to your good life for ever.

M.F. What shall I do? There is a gentleman my dear
friend; and I fear not mine own shame so much, as
his peril. I had rather than a thousand pound he 110
were out of the house.

M.P. For shame! never stand; ('you had rather' and
'you had rather'!) your husband's here at hand;
bethink you of some conveyance: in the house you
cannot hide him. O, how have you deceiv'd me!
Look, here is a basket, if he be of any reasonable
stature, he may creep in here, and throw foul linen
upon him, as if it were going to bucking: or,—it is
whiting-time,—send him by your two men to
Datchet Mead. 120

M.F. He's too big to go in there. What shall I do?

Fal. (*coming forward*) Let me see't, let me see't, O, let
me see't!—I'll in, I'll in.—Follow your friend's
counsel.—I'll in.

M.P. What, Sir John Falstaff? Are these your letters,
knight?

Fal. I love thee.—Help me away.—Let me creep in here.
—I'll never—

     Gets into the basket; they cover him with foul linen

M.P. Help to cover your master, boy.—Call your men,
Mistress Ford.—You dissembling knight! 130

M.F. What, John! Robert! John!   *Exit Robin*

Re-enter Servants

Go, take up these clothes here, quickly.—Where's the cowl-staff? look how you drumble!—Carry them to the laundress in Datchet Mead; quickly, come.

Enter Ford, Page, Caius, and Sir Hugh Evans

Fo. Pray you come near: if I suspect without cause, why then make sport at me, then let me be your jest, I deserve it.—How now? whither bear you this?

Ser. To the laundress, forsooth.   140

M.F. Why, what have you to do whither they bear it? You were best meddle with buck-washing!

Fo. Buck?—I would I could wash myself of the buck! —Buck, buck, buck, ay, buck; I warrant you, buck; and of the season too; it shall appear. (*exeunt Servants with the basket.*)   Gentlemen, I have dream'd to-night, I'll tell you my dream.   Here, here, here be my keys, ascend my chambers, search, seek, find out: I'll warrant we'll unkennel the fox.   Let me stop this way first. (*Locking the door.*)   So, now   150 uncape.   †

Pa. Good Master Ford, be contented: you wrong yourself too much.

67

Fo. True, Master Page. Up, gentlemen, you shall see
sport anon: follow me, gentlemen.   *Exit*

Ev. This is fery fantastical humours and jealousies.

Cai. By gar, 'tis no the fashion of France; it is not jealous
in France.

Pa. Nay, follow him, gentlemen, see the issue of his
search.   160

Exeunt Page, Caius, and Evans

M.P. Is there not a double excellency in this?

M.F. I know not which pleases me better, that my husband is deceiv'd, or Sir John.

M.P. What a taking was he in, when your husband ask'd
who was in the basket!

M.F. I am half afraid he will have need of washing; so
throwing him into the water will do him a benefit.

M.P. Hang him, dishonest rascal! I would all of the
same strain were in the same distress.

M.F. I think my husband hath some special suspicion of   170
Falstaff's being here; for I never saw him so gross
in his jealousy till now.

M.P. I will lay a plot to try that, and we will yet have more
tricks with Falstaff: his dissolute disease will scarce
obey this medicine.

M.F. Shall we send that foolish carrion, Mistress Quickly,
to him, and excuse his throwing into the water,

and give him another hope, to betray him to another
punishment?

M.P. We will do it: let him be sent for to-morrow eight 180
o'clock, to have amends.

Re-enter Ford, Page, Caius, and Sir Hugh Evans

Fo. I cannot find him: may be the knave bragg'd of
that he could not compass.

M.P. (*aside to Mrs Ford*) Heard you that?

M.F. You use me well, Master Ford, do you?

Fo. Ay, I do so.

M.F. Heaven make you better than your thoughts!

Fo. Amen!

M.P. You do yourself mighty wrong, Master Ford.

Fo. Ay, ay; I must bear it.   190

Ev. By Jeshu, if there be any pody in the house, and in
the chambers, and in the coffers, and in the presses,
heaven forgive my sins at the day of judgement!

Cai. By gar, nor I too: there is no bodies.

Pa. Fie, fie, Master Ford! are you not asham'd?   What
spirit, what devil suggests this imagination?   I
would not ha' your distemper in this kind for the
wealth of Windsor Castle.

Fo. 'Tis my fault, Master Page: I suffer for it.

Ev. You suffer for a pad conscience: your wife is as 200

honest a 'omans as I will desires among five
thousand, and five hundred too.

Cai. By gar, I see 'tis an honest woman.

Fo. Well, I promis'd you a dinner. Come, come, walk
in the park, I pray you pardon me ; I will hereafter
make known to you why I have done this. Come,
wife, come, Mistress Page, I pray you pardon me ;
pray heartily pardon me.

Pa. Let's go in, gentlemen, but, trust me, we'll mock
him. I do invite you to-morrow morning to my 210
house to breakfast : after, we'll a-birding together ;
I have a fine hawk for the bush. Shall it be so ?

Fo. Any thing.

Ev. If there is one, I shall make two in the company.

Cai. If there be one, or two, I shall make-a the turd.

Fo. Pray you, go, Master Page.

Ev. I pray you now, remembrance to-morrow on the
lousy knave, mine host.

Cai. Dat is good, by gar, with all my heart.

Ev. A lousy knave, to have his gibes, and his mockeries ! 220

Exeunt

SCENE IV

A room in Page's house

Enter Fenton and Anne Page

Fen. I see I cannot get thy father's love ;
    Therefore no more turn me to him, sweet Nan.

An. Alas, how then ?

Fen.   Why, thou must be thyself.
    He doth object, I am too great of birth,
    And that, my state being gall'd with my expense,
    I seek to heal it only by his wealth :
    Besides these, other bars he lays before me,
    My riots past, my wild societies,
    And tells me 'tis a thing impossible
    I should love thee, but as a property.   10

An. May be he tells you true.

Fen. No, heaven so speed me in my time to come !
    Albeit I will confess, thy father's wealth
    Was the first motive that I woo'd thee, Anne :
    Yet, wooing thee, I found thee of more value
    Than stamps in gold, or sums in sealed bags ;
    And 'tis the very riches of thyself
    That now I aim at.

An.   Gentle Master Fenton,

> Yet seek my father's love, still seek it, sir ;
> If opportunity and humblest suit   20
> Cannot attain it, why, then,—hark you hither !

They converse apart

Enter Shallow, Slender, and Mistress Quickly

Sha. Break their talk, Mistress Quickly : my kinsman shall speak for himself.

Sle. I 'll make a shaft or a bolt on 't : 'slid, 'tis but venturing.

Sha. Be not dismay'd.

Sle. No, she shall not dismay me : I care not for that, but that I am afeard.

M.Q. Hark ye, Master Slender would speak a word with you.   30

An. I come to him. (*aside*) This is my father's choice. O, what a world of vile ill-favour'd faults Looks handsome in three hundred pounds a-year !

M.Q. And how does good Master Fenton ? Pray you, a word with you.

Sha. She 's coming ; to her, coz. O boy, thou hadst a father !

Sle. I had a father, Mistress Anne, my uncle can tell you good jests of him. Pray you, uncle, tell Mistress Anne the jest how my father stole two geese out of † a pen, good uncle.   41

72

Sha. Mistress Anne, my cousin loves you.

Sle. Ay, that I do, as well as I love any woman in Gloucestershire.

Sha. He will maintain you like a gentlewoman.

Sle. Ay, that I will, come cut and long-tail, under the degree of a squire.

Sha. He will make you a hundred and fifty pounds jointure.

An. Good Master Shallow, let him woo for himself.   50

Sha. Marry, I thank you for it ; I thank you for that good comfort.   She calls you, coz, I 'll leave you.

An. Now, Master Slender,—

Sle. Now, good Mistress Anne,—

An. What is your will ?

Sle. My will ? od 's heartlings, that 's a pretty jest indeed !   I ne'er made my will yet, I thank heaven ; I am not such a sickly creature, I give heaven praise.

An. I mean, Master Slender, what would you with me ?

Sle. Truly, for mine own part, I would little or nothing   60
with you : your father and my uncle hath made motions : if it be my luck, so ; if not, happy man be his dole !   They can tell you how things go, better than I can : you may ask your father, here he comes.

Enter Page and Mistress Page

Pa. Now, Master Slender : love him, daughter Anne.—

73

Why, how now ? what does Master Fenton here ?
You wrong me, sir, thus still to haunt my house :
I told you, sir, my daughter is dispos'd of.

Fen. Nay, Master Page, be not impatient.

M.P. Good Master Fenton, come not to my child.   70

Pa. She is no match for you.

Fen. Sir, will you hear me ?

Pa.   No, good Master Fenton.
Come, Master Shallow ; come, son Slender, in.
Knowing my mind, you wrong me, Master Fenton.
     Exeunt Page, Shallow, and Slender

M.Q. Speak to Mistress Page.

Fen. Good Mistress Page, for that I love your daughter
In such a righteous fashion as I do,
Perforce, against all checks, rebukes, and manners,
I must advance the colours of my love,
And not retire : let me have your good will.   80

An. Good mother, do not marry me to yond fool.

M.P. I mean it not, I seek you a better husband.

M.Q. That 's my master, master doctor.

An. Alas, I had rather be set quick i' the earth,
And bowl'd to death with turnips !

M.P. Come, trouble not yourself, good Master Fenton,
I will not be your friend, nor enemy :
My daughter will I question how she loves you,

And as I find her, so am I affected.

Till then, farewell, sir, she must needs go in,   90

Her father will be angry,

Fen. Farewell, gentle mistress : farewell, Nan.

Exeunt Mrs Page and Anne

M.Q. This is my doing now : ' Nay,' said I, ' will you
cast away your child on a fool, and a physician ?
Look on Master Fenton : ' this is my doing.

Fen. I thank thee ; and I pray thee once to-night
Give my sweet Nan this ring : there's for thy pains.

M.Q. Now heaven send thee good fortune ! (*exit
Fenton.*) A kind heart he hath : a woman would
run through fire and water for such a kind heart. 100
But yet I would my master had Mistress Anne, or I
would Master Slender had her ; or, in sooth, I would
Master Fenton had her : I will do what I can for
them all three, for so I have promis'd, and I'll be
as good as my word, but speciously for Master
Fenton.   Well, I must of another errand to Sir
John Falstaff from my two mistresses : what a beast
am I to slack it !   *Exit*

SCENE V

A room in the Garter Inn

Enter Falstaff and Bardolph

Fal. Bardolph, I say,—

Bar. Here, sir.

Fal. Go fetch me a quart of sack, put a toast in 't. (*exit
Bardolph.*)   Have I liv'd to be carried in a basket,
like a barrow of butcher's offal? and to be thrown
in the Thames?   Well, if I be serv'd such another
trick, I 'll have my brains ta'en out and butter'd, and
give them to a dog for a new-year's gift.   The rogues
slighted me into the river with as little remorse, as
they would have drown'd a blind bitch's puppies,   10
fifteen i' the litter: and you may know by my size,
that I have a kind of alacrity in sinking; if the
bottom were as deep as hell, I should down.   I had
been drown'd, but that the shore was shelvy and
shallow; a death that I abhor; for the water swells
a man; and what a thing should I have been, when
I had been swell'd!   I should have been a mountain
of mummy.

Re-enter Bardolph with sack

Bar. Here 's Mistress Quickly, sir, to speak with you.

Fal. Come, let me pour in some sack to the Thames   20
     water ; for my belly 's as cold as if I had swallow'd
     snowballs, for pills to cool the reins.   Call her in.

Bar. Come in, woman !

Enter Mrs Quickly

M.Q. By your leave ; I cry you mercy : give your wor-
     ship good morrow.

Fal. Take away these chalices.   Go, brew me a pottle of
     sack finely.

Bar. With eggs, sir ?

Fal. Simple of itself ; I 'll no pullet-sperm in my brewage.
     (*exit Bardolph.*)   How now ?   30

M.Q. Marry, sir, I come to your worship from Mistress
     Ford.

Fal. Mistress Ford ?   I have had ford enough ; I was
     thrown into the ford ; I have my belly full of ford.

M.Q. Alas the day ! good heart, that was not her fault :
     she does so take on with her men ; they mistook
     their erection.

Fal. So did I mine, to build upon a foolish woman's
     promise.

M.Q. Well, she laments, sir, for it, that it would yearn your   40
     heart to see it.   Her husband goes this morning a-
     birding ; she desires you once more to come to her,

between eight and nine: I must carry her word quickly, she 'll make you amends, I warrant you.

Fal. Well, I will visit her, tell her so; and bid her think what a man is: let her consider his frailty, and then judge of my merit.

M.Q. I will tell her.

Fal. Do so. Between nine and ten, sayst thou?

M.Q. Eight and nine, sir.   50

Fal. Well, be gone: I will not miss her.

M.Q. Peace be with you, sir.   *Exit*

Fal. I marvel I hear not of Master Brook; he sent me word to stay within: I like his money well.—By the mass, here he comes.

Enter Ford

Fo. God save you, sir!

Fal. Now, Master Brook,—you come to know what hath passed between me, and Ford's wife?

Fo. That, indeed, Sir John, is my business.

Fal. Master Brook, I will not lie to you, I was at her house   60
the hour she appointed me.

Fo. And sped you, sir?

Fal. Very ill-favouredly, Master Brook.

Fo. How so, sir? Did she change her determination?

Fal. No, Master Brook; but the peaking Cornuto her husband, Master Brook, dwelling in a continual

'larum of jealousy, comes me in the instant of our
encounter, after we had embrac'd, kiss'd, protested,
and, as it were, spoke the prologue of our comedy;
and at his heels, a rabble of his companions, thither   70
provoked and instigated by his distemper, and (forsooth) to search his house for his wife's love.

Fo. What?   While you were there?

Fal. While I was there.

Fo. And did he search for you, and could not find you?

Fal. You shall hear.   As good luck would have it, comes
in one Mistress Page, gives intelligence of Ford's
approach; and in her invention, and Ford's wife's
distraction, they convey'd me into a buck-basket.

Fo. A buck-basket?   80

Fal. By the Lord, a buck-basket!—ramm'd me in with foul
shirts and smocks, socks, foul stockings, greasy nap-
kins, that, Master Brook, there was the rankest com-
pound of villanous smell, that ever offended nostril.

Fo. And how long lay you there?

Fal. Nay, you shall hear, Master Brook, what I have
suffer'd, to bring this woman to evil, for your good.
Being thus cramm'd in the basket, a couple of Ford's
knaves, his hinds, were called forth by their mistress,   90
to carry me in the name of foul clothes to Datchet-
lane: they took me on their shoulders; met the

jealous knave their master in the door; who ask'd them once or twice what they had in their basket: I quak'd for fear lest the lunatic knave would have search'd it; but fate (ordaining he should be a cuckold) held his hand. Well, on went he, for a search, and away went I for foul clothes. But mark the sequel, Master Brook: I suffered the pangs of three several deaths; first, an intolerable fright, to 100 be detected with a jealous rotten bell-wether; next, to be compass'd like a good bilbo in the circumference of a peck, hilt to point, heel to head; and then, to be stopp'd in like a strong distillation with stinking clothes, that fretted in their own grease: think of that, a man of my kidney; think of that, that am as subject to heat as butter; a man of continual dissolution, and thaw: it was a miracle to 'scape suffocation. And in the height of this bath, when I was more than half stew'd in grease (like a Dutch 110 dish) to be thrown into the Thames, and cool'd, glowing hot, in that surge, like a horse-shoe; think of that; hissing hot; think of that, Master Brook.

Fo. In good sadness, sir, I am sorry that for my sake you have suffer'd all this. My suit, then, is desperate; you 'll undertake her no more?

Fal. Master Brook, I will be thrown into Etna, as I have

been into Thames, ere I will leave her thus. Her
husband is this morning gone a-birding: I have
receiv'd from her another embassy of meeting; 120
'twixt eight and nine is the hour, Master Brook.

Fo. 'Tis past eight already, sir.

Fal. Is it? I will then address me to my appointment.
Come to me at your convenient leisure, and you
shall know how I speed; and the conclusion shall
be crown'd with your enjoying her. Adieu. You
shall have her, Master Brook; Master Brook, you
shall cuckold Ford.   *Exit*

Fo. Hum! ha! is this a vision? is this a dream? do I
sleep? Master Ford, awake! awake, Master Ford! 130
there's a hole made in your best coat, Master
Ford. This 'tis to be married! this 'tis to have
linen, and buck-baskets! Well, I will proclaim
myself what I am: I will now take the lecher; he
is at my house; he cannot 'scape me; 'tis impossible he should; he cannot creep into a half-penny
purse, nor into a pepper-box: but, lest the devil
that guides him should aid him, I will search impossible places. Though what I am I cannot avoid,
yet to be what I would not shall not make me tame: 140
if I have horns, to make one mad, let the proverb
go with me,—I'll be horn-mad.   *Exit*

Act Fourth

A street

Enter Mistress Page, Mistress Quickly, and William

M.P. Is he at Master Ford's already, think'st thou ?

M.Q. Sure he is by this ; or will be presently : but, truly, he is very courageous mad, about his throwing into the water. Mistress Ford desires you to come suddenly.

M.P. I 'll be with her by and by : I 'll but bring my young man here to school. Look where his master comes ; 'tis a playing-day, I see.

Enter Sir Hugh Evans

How now, Sir Hugh, no school to-day ?

Ev. No ; Master Slender is let the boys leave to play.   10

M.Q. Blessing of his heart !

M.P. Sir Hugh, my husband says my son profits nothing in the world at his book. I pray you ask him some questions in his accidence.

Ev. Come hither, William ; hold up your head ; come.

*M.P.*Come on, sirrah ; hold up your head ; answer
   your master, be not afraid.

Ev. William, how many numbers is in nouns ?

Wil. Two.

*M.Q.*Truly, I thought there had been one number more,   20
   because they say, ' Od 's nouns.'

Ev. Peace your tattlings !   What is ' fair,' William ?

Wil. Pulcher.

*M.Q.*Polecats ?   there are fairer things than polecats,
   sure.

Ev. You are a very simplicity 'oman : I pray you peace.
   —What is *lapis*, William ?

Wil. A stone.

Ev. And what is ' a stone,' William ?

Wil. A pebble.   30

Ev. No ; it is *lapis* : I pray you remember in your
   prain.

Wil. Lapis.

Ev. That is a good William.   What is he, William, that
   does lend articles ?

Wil. Articles are borrow'd of the pronoun ; and be thus
   declin'd, *Singulariter, nominatiuo, hic, hæc, hoc.*

Ev. Nominatiuo, hig, hag, hog ; pray you mark : *genitivo,
   huius.*   Well, what is your accusative case ?

Wil. Accusativo hinc.   40

83

Ev. I pray you, have your remembrance, child ; *accusativo,
 hung, hang, hog.*

M.Q. ' Hang-hog ' is Latin for bacon, I warrant you.

Ev. Leave your prabbles, 'oman.—What is the focative
 case, William ?

Wil. O,—vocativo, O.

Ev. Remember, William ; focative is *caret.*

M.Q. And that 's a good root.

Ev. 'Oman, forbear.

M.P. Peace !   50

Ev. What is your genitive case plural, William ?

Wil. Genitive case ?

Ev. Ay.

Wil. Genitivo,—horum, harum, horum.

M.Q. Vengeance of Jinny's case ! fie on her ! never name
 her, child, if she be a whore.

Ev. For shame, 'oman.

M.Q. You do ill to teach the child such words : he teaches
 him to hick and to hack ; which they 'll do fast
 enough of themselves, and to call ' horum ' :—fie   60
 upon you !

Ev. 'Oman, art thou lunaties ? hast thou no under-
 standings for thy cases, and the numbers of the
 genders ? Thou art as foolish Christian creatures
 as I would desires.

M.P. Prithee hold thy peace.

Ev. Show me now, William, some declensions of your
    pronouns.

Wil. Forsooth, I have forgot.

Ev. It is *qui*, *quæ*, *quod* : if you forget your ' quis,' your   70
    ' quæs,' and your ' quods,' you must be preeches.
    Go your ways and play, go.

M.P. He is a better scholar than I thought he was.

Ev. He is a good sprag memory. Farewell, Mistress
    Page.

M.P. Adieu, good Sir Hugh.   *Exit Sir Hugh*

    Get you home, boy.   Come, we stay too long.

                                            Exeunt

SCENE II

A room in Ford's house

Enter Falstaff and Mistress Ford

Fal. Mistress Ford, your sorrow hath eaten up my suffer-
    ance ; I see you are obsequious in your love, and I
    profess requital to a hair's breadth, not only, Mistress
    Ford, in the simple office of love, but in all the
    accoutrement, complement, and ceremony of it.
    But are you sure of your husband now ?

*M.F.*He's a-birding, sweet Sir John.

M.P.(*within*) What ho, gossip Ford! what ho!

*M.F.*Step into the chamber, Sir John.   *Exit Falstaff*

Enter Mistress Page

*M.P.*How now, sweetheart? who's at home besides   10
     yourself?

*M.F.*Why, none but mine own people.

*M.P.*Indeed!

*M.F.*No, certainly. (*aside to her*) Speak louder.

*M.P.*Truly, I am so glad you have nobody here.

*M.F.*Why?

*M.P.*Why, woman, your husband is in his old lines †
     again: he so takes on yonder with my husband,
     so rails against all married mankind; so curses all
     Eve's daughters, of what complexion soever; and   20
     so buffets himself on the forehead, crying, 'Peer
     out, peer out!' that any madness I ever yet beheld
     seem'd but tameness, civility, and patience to this
     his distemper he is in now: I am glad the fat knight
     is not here.

*M.F.*Why, does he talk of him?

*M.P.*Of none but him, and swears he was carried out
     the last time he search'd for him, in a basket; pro-
     tests to my husband he is now here, and hath drawn
     him and the rest of their company from their sport,   30

to make another experiment of his suspicion : but
I am glad the knight is not here ; now he shall see
his own foolery.

M.F. How near is he, Mistress Page ?

M.P. Hard by, at street end ; he will be here anon.

M.F. I am undone, the knight is here.

M.P. Why then, you are utterly sham'd, and he 's but a
dead man.   What a woman are you !   Away with
him, away with him !   better shame, than murder.

M.F. Which way should he go ?   how should I bestow   40
him ?   Shall I put him into the basket again ?

Re-enter Falstaff

Fal. No, I 'll come no more i' the basket.   May I not go
out ere he come ?

M.P. Alas, three of Master Ford's brothers watch the
door with pistols, that none shall issue out ; otherwise you might slip away ere he came.   But what
make you here ?

Fal. What shall I do ?   I 'll creep up into the chimney.

M.F. There they always use to discharge their birding-
pieces.   Creep into the kiln-hole.   50

Fal. Where is it ?

M.F. He will seek there, on my word.   Neither press,
coffer, chest, trunk, well, vault, but he hath an

abstract for the remembrance of such places, and
goes to them by his note : there is no hiding you
in the house.

Fal. I 'll go out, then.

M.F. If you go out in your own semblance, you die, Sir
John, unless you go out disguis'd,—how might we
disguise him ?   60

M.P. Alas the day, I know not ! There is no woman's
gown big enough for him ; otherwise he might put
on a hat, a muffler, and a kerchief, and so escape.

Fal. For God's sake, devise something : any extremity,
rather than a mischief.

M.F. My maid's aunt, the fat woman of Brentford, has
a gown above.

M.P. On my word, it will serve him ; she 's as big as
he is : and there 's her thrumm'd hat, and her
muffler too. Run up, Sir John.   70

M.F. Go, go, sweet Sir John : Mistress Page and I will
look some linen for your head.

M.P. Quick, quick ! we 'll come dress you straight : put
on the gown the while.   *Exit Falstaff*

M.F. I would my husband would meet him in this shape :
he cannot abide the old woman of Brentford ; he
swears she 's a witch, forbade her my house, and
hath threaten'd to beat her.

*M.P.*Heaven guide him to thy husband's cudgel; and
   the devil guide his cudgel afterwards!   80

*M.F.*But is my husband coming?

*M.P.*Ay, in good sadness, is he, and talks of the basket
   too, howsoever he hath had intelligence.

*M.F.*We'll try that; for I'll appoint my men to carry
   the basket again, to meet him at the door with it, as
   they did last time.

*M.P.*Nay, but he'll be here presently: let's go dress
   him like the witch of Brentford.

*M.F.*I'll first direct my men, what they shall do with the
   basket.   Go up, I'll bring linen for him straight.   90
                                                        Exit

*M.P.*Hang him, dishonest varlet! we cannot misuse
   him enough.
      We'll leave a proof, by that which we will do,
      Wives may be merry, and yet honest too:
      We do not act that often jest and laugh,
      'Tis old, but true, still swine eats all the draff. *Exit*
         Re-enter Mistress Ford with two Servants

*M.F.*Go, sirs, take the basket again on your shoulders:
   your master is hard at door; if he bid you set it
   down, obey him: quickly, dispatch.   *Exit*

1.S. Come, come, take it up.   100

2.S. Pray heaven it be not full of knight again.

1.*S.* I hope not, I had as lief bear so much lead.

    Enter Ford, Page, Shallow, Caius, and Sir Hugh Evans

Fo. Ay, but if it prove true, Master Page, have you any
    way then to unfool me again? Set down the basket,
    villain! Somebody call my wife. Youth in a
    basket! O you pandarly rascals, there's a knot;
    a ging, a pack, a conspiracy against me: now shall
    the devil be sham'd.—What, wife, I say! Come,
    come forth! Behold what honest clothes you send 110
    forth to bleaching!

Pa. Why, this passes, Master Ford; you are not to go
    loose any longer, you must be pinion'd.

Ev. Why, this is lunatics! this is mad, as a mad dog!

Sha. Indeed, Master Ford, this is not well, indeed.

Fo. So say I too, sir.

    Re-enter Mistress Ford

    Come hither, Mistress Ford, Mistress Ford, the
    honest woman, the modest wife, the virtuous crea-
    ture, that hath the jealous fool to her husband! I
    suspect without cause, mistress, do I? 120

M.F. Ay, God's my record, do you, if you suspect me in
    any dishonesty.

Fo. Well said, brazen-face! hold it out. Come forth,
    sirrah!   *Pulling clothes out of the basket*

Pa. This passes!

M.F. Are you not asham'd ? let the clothes alone.

Fo. I shall find you anon.

Ev. 'Tis unreasonable ! Will you take up your wife's clothes ? Come, away.

Fo. Empty the basket, I say !   130

M.F. Why, man, why ?

Fo. Master Page, as I am a man, there was one convey'd out of my house yesterday in this basket : why may not he be there again ?   In my house I am sure he is : my intelligence is true, my jealousy is reasonable, pluck me out all the linen.

M.F. If you find a man there, he shall die a flea's death.

Pa. Here's no man.

Sha. By my fidelity, this is not well, Master Ford ; this wrongs you.   140

Ev. Master Ford, you must pray, and not follow the imaginations of your own heart : this is jealousies.

Fo. Well, he's not here I seek for.

Pa. No, nor nowhere else but in your brain.

Fo. Help to search my house this one time. If I find not what I seek, show no colour for my extremity ; let me for ever be your table-sport ; let them say of me, ' As jealous as Ford, that searched a hollow walnut for his wife's leman.'   Satisfy me once more, once more search with me.   150

*M.F.*What, ho, Mistress Page! come you and the old
woman down; my husband will come into the
chamber.

Fo. Old woman? what old woman's that?

*M.F.*Why, it is my maid's aunt of Brentford.

Fo. A witch, a quean, an old cozening quean! Have I
not forbid her my house? She comes of errands,
does she? We are simple men, we do not know
what's brought to pass under the profession of
fortune-telling. She works by charms, by spells, by 160
the figure, and such daubery as this is, beyond our
element: we know nothing. Come down, you
witch, you hag, you, come down, I say!

*M.F.*Nay, good sweet husband!—Good gentlemen, let
him not strike the old woman.

Re-enter Falstaff in woman's clothes, and Mistress Page

*M.P.*Come, Mother Prat, come, give me your hand.

Fo. I'll prat her. (*Beating him*) Out of my door, you
witch, you rag, you baggage, you polecat, you
ronyon! out, out! I'll conjure you, I'll fortune-
tell you.   *Exit Falstaff* 170

*M.P.*Are you not asham'd? I think you have kill'd the
poor woman.

*M.F.*Nay, he will do it, 'tis a goodly credit for you.

Fo. Hang her, witch!

Ev. (*aside*) By yea and no, I think the 'oman is a witch
  indeed : I like not when a 'oman has a great peard ;
  I spy a great peard under his muffler.

Fo. Will you follow, gentlemen ? I beseech you, follow ;
  see but the issue of my jealousy : if I cry out thus
  upon no trail, never trust me when I open again.   180

Pa. Let 's obey his humour a little further : come,
  gentlemen.

  Exeunt Ford, Page, Shallow, Caius, and Evans

M.P. Trust me, he beat him most pitifully.

M.F. Nay, by the mass, that he did not ; he beat him
  most unpitifully, methought.

M.P. I 'll have the cudgel hallow'd, and hung o'er the
  altar ; it hath done meritorious service.

M.F. What think you ? may we, with the warrant of
  womanhood, and the witness of a good conscience,
  pursue him with any further revenge ?   190

M.P. The spirit of wantonness is sure scar'd out of him,
  if the devil have him not in fee-simple, with fine and
  recovery, he will never, I think, in the way of waste,
  attempt us again.

M.F. Shall we tell our husbands how we have serv'd him ?

M.P. Yes, by all means ; if it be but to scrape the figures
  out of your husband's brains. If they can find in
  their hearts the poor unvirtuous fat knight shall

be any further afflicted, we two will still be the
ministers.   200

M.F. I 'll warrant they 'll have him publicly sham'd, and
methinks there would be no period to the jest,
should he not be publicly sham'd.

M.P. Come, to the forge with it, then shape it : I would
not have things cool.   *Exeunt*

SCENE III

A room in the Garter Inn

Enter Host and Bardolph

Bar. Sir, the Germans desire to have three of your horses :
the duke himself will be to-morrow at court, and
they are going to meet him.

Ho. What duke should that be comes so secretly ? I
hear not of him in the court. Let me speak with the
gentlemen ; they speak English ?

Bar. Ay, sir ; I 'll call them to you.

Ho. They shall have my horses, but I 'll make them
pay ; I 'll sauce them, they have had my house a
week at command ; I have turn'd away my other   10
guests : they must come off, I 'll sauce them ; come.
                                                        Exeunt

SCENE IV

A room in Ford's house

Enter Page, Ford, Mistress Page, Mistress Ford,
and Sir Hugh Evans

Ev. 'Tis one of the best discretions of a 'oman as ever
    I did look upon.

Pa. And did he send you both these letters at an instant?

M.P. Within a quarter of an hour.

Fo. Pardon me, wife. Henceforth do what thou wilt;
    I rather will suspect the sun with cold
    Than thee with wantonness: now doth thy honour
        stand,
    In him that was of late an heretic,
    As firm as faith.

Pa.   'Tis well, 'tis well, no more:
    Be not as extreme in submission   10
    As in offence.
    But let our plot go forward: let our wives
    Yet once again, to make us public sport,
    Appoint a meeting with this old fat fellow,
    Where we may take him, and disgrace him for it.

Fo. There is no better way than that they spoke of.

Pa. How? to send him word they'll meet him in the
    Park at midnight? Fie, fie! he'll never come.

Ev. You say he has been thrown in the rivers; and has
    been grievously peaten, as an old 'oman: methinks   20
    there should be terrors in him, that he should not
    come; methinks his flesh is punish'd, he shall have
    no desires.

Pa. So think I too.

*M.F.*Devise but how you'll use him when he comes,
    And let us two devise to bring him thither.

*M.P.*There is an old tale goes, that Herne the hunter,   †
    Sometime a keeper here in Windsor forest,
    Doth all the winter-time, at still midnight,
    Walk round about an oak, with great ragg'd horns;   30
    And there he blasts the tree, and takes the cattle,
    And makes milch-kine yield blood, and shakes a chain
    In a most hideous and dreadful manner:
    You have heard of such a spirit, and well you know
    The superstitious idle-headed eld
    Receiv'd, and did deliver to our age,
    This tale of Herne the hunter, for a truth.

Pa. Why, yet there want not many that do fear
    In deep of night to walk by this Herne's oak:
    But what of this?

M.F.   Marry, this is our device,   4

That Falstaff at that oak shall meet with us.
[Disguis'd like Herne, with huge horns in his head.]
Pa. Well, let it not be doubted but he 'll come,
And in this shape, when you have brought him thither,
What shall be done with him ? what is your plot ?
M.P. That likewise have we thought upon, and thus :
Nan Page, my daughter, and my little son,
And three or four more of their growth, we 'll dress
Like urchins, ouphs, and fairies, green and white,
With rounds of waxen tapers on their heads,   50
And rattles in their hands : upon a sudden,
As Falstaff, she, and I, are newly met,
Let them from forth a sawpit rush at once
With some diffused song : upon their sight,
We two in great amazedness will fly :
Then let them all encircle him about,
And fairy-like to pinch the unclean knight ;
And ask him, why that hour of fairy revel,
In their so sacred paths, he dares to tread
In shape profane.
M.F.   And till he tell the truth,   60
Let the supposed fairies pinch him sound,
And burn him with their tapers.
M.P.   The truth being known,
We 'll all present ourselves, dis-horn the spirit,

97

And mock him home to Windsor.

Fo.   The children must
Be practis'd well to this, or they 'll ne'er do 't.

Ev. I will teach the children their behaviours ; and I
will be like a jack-an-apes also, to burn the knight
with my taber.

Fo. That will be excellent ; I 'll go buy them vizards.

M.P. My Nan shall be the queen of all the fairies,   70
Finely attired in a robe of white.

Pa. That silk will I go buy. (*aside*) And in that time.
Shall Master Slender steal my Nan away,
And marry her at Eton. Go, send to Falstaff straight.

Fo. Nay, I 'll to him again in name of Brook :
He 'll tell me all his purpose : sure he 'll come.

M.P. Fear not you that. Go get us properties
And tricking for our fairies.

Ev. Let us about it, it is admirable pleasures and fery
honest knaveries.   *Exeunt Page, Ford, and Evans* 80

M.P. Go, Mistress Ford,
Send quickly to Sir John, to know his mind.

            Exit Mrs Ford

I 'll to the doctor, he hath my good will,
And none but he, to marry with Nan Page.
That Slender, though well landed, is an idiot ;
And he my husband best of all affects.

The doctor is well money'd, and his friends
Potent at court : he, none but he, shall have her,
Though twenty thousand worthier come to crave her.

Exit

SCENES V AND VI

The Garter Inn

Enter Host and Simple

Ho. What wouldst thou have, boor ? what, thickskin ?
 speak, breathe, discuss ; brief, short, quick, snap.

Sim. Marry, sir, I come to speak with Sir John Falstaff
 from Master Slender.

Ho. There's his chamber, his house, his castle, his
 standing-bed and truckle-bed ; 'tis painted about
 with the story of the Prodigal, fresh and new.   Go,
 knock and call ; he'll speak like an Anthropophaginian unto thee : knock, I say.

Sim. There's an old woman, a fat woman, gone up into   10
 his chamber : I'll be so bold as stay, sir, till she
 come down ; I come to speak with her, indeed.

Ho. Ha ! a fat woman ? the knight may be robb'd : I'll
 call.—Bully knight ! bully Sir John ! speak from
 thy lungs military : art thou there ? it is thine host,
 thine Ephesian, calls.

Fal. (*above*) How now, mine host?

Ho. Here's a Bohemian-Tartar tarries the coming down
of thy fat woman. Let her descend, bully, let her
descend; my chambers are honourable: fie!   20
privacy? fie!

Enter Falstaff

Fal. There was, mine host, an old fat woman even now
with me, but she's gone.

Sim. Pray you, sir, was't not the wise woman of Brentford?

Fal. Ay, marry, was it, mussel-shell, what would you
with her?

Sim. My master, sir, Master Slender, sent to her, seeing
her go thorough the streets, to know, sir, whether
one Nym, sir, that beguil'd him of a chain, had the   30
chain or no.

Fal. I spake with the old woman about it.

Sim. And what says she, I pray, sir?

Fal. Marry, she says, that the very same man that beguil'd
Master Slender of his chain, cozen'd him of it.

Sim. I would I could have spoken with the woman herself, I had other things to have spoken with her
too, from him.

Fal. What are they? let us know.

Ho. Ay, come, quick.   40

Sim. I may not conceal them, sir.

Ho. Conceal them, or thou diest.

Sim. Why, sir, they were nothing but about Mistress Anne Page, to know if it were my master's fortune to have her, or no.

Fal. 'Tis, 'tis his fortune.

Sim. What, sir?

Fal. To have her, or no : go ; say the woman told me so.

Sim. May I be bold to say so, sir?

Fal. Ay, tyke, who more bold?   †

Sim. I thank your worship : I shall make my master glad   51
with these tidings.   *Exit*

Ho. Thou art clerkly ; thou art clerkly, Sir John.   Was there a wise woman with thee?

Fal. Ay, that there was, mine host, one that hath taught me more wit than ever I learn'd before in my life ; and I paid nothing for it neither, but was paid for my learning.

Enter Bardolph

Bar. Out, alas, sir! cozenage, mere cozenage!

Ho. Where be my horses? speak well of them, varletto.   60

Bar. Run away with the cozeners : for so soon as I came beyond Eton, they threw me off, from behind one of them, in a slough of mire ; and set spurs, and

away; like three German devils; three Doctor
Faustuses.

Ho. They are gone but to meet the duke, villain: do not
say they be fled; Germans are honest men.

Enter Sir Hugh Evans

Ev. Where is mine host?

Ho. What is the matter, sir?

Ev. Have a care of your entertainments: there is a 70
friend of mine come to town, tells me there is three
cozen-germans, that has cozen'd all the hosts of †
Readins, of Maidenhead, of Colebrook, of horses
and money. I tell you for good will, look you:
you are wise, and full of gibes and vlouting-stocks,
and 'tis not convenient you should be cozen'd.
Fare you well. *Exit*

Enter Doctor Caius

Cai. Vere is mine host de Jarteer?

Ho. Here, master doctor, in perplexity, and doubtful
dilemma. 80

Cai. I cannot tell vat is dat: but it is tell-a me dat you
make grand preparation for a duke de Jamany: by
my trot', dere is no duke dat the court is know, to
come. I tell you for good vill: adieu. *Exit*

Ho. Hue and cry, villain, go! Assist me, knight, I am

undone !   Fly, run, hue and cry, villain !   I am
undone !   *Exeunt Host and Bardolph*

Fal. I would all the world might be cozen'd, for I have
been cozen'd and beaten too.   If it should come to
the ear of the court, how I have been transform'd,   90
and how my transformation hath been wash'd and
cudgell'd, they would melt me out of my fat drop
by drop, and liquor fishermen's boots with me : I
warrant they would whip me with their fine wits, till
I were as crest-fallen as a dried pear.   I never prosper'd, since I forswore myself at primero.   Well, if
my wind were but long enough [to say my prayers],
I would repent.

Enter Mistress Quickly

Now, whence come you ?

M.Q. From the two parties, forsooth.   100

Fal. The devil take one party, and his dam the other !
and so they shall be both bestow'd.   I have suffer'd
more for their sakes, more than the villanous incon-
stancy of man's disposition is able to bear.

M.Q. And have not they suffer'd ?   Yes, I warrant ;
speciously one of them ; Mistress Ford, good heart,
is beaten black and blue, that you cannot see a
white spot about her.

Fal. What tell'st thou me of black, and blue ?   I was

beaten myself into all the colours of the rainbow; 110
and I was like to be apprehended for the witch of
Brentford, but that my admirable dexterity of wit, my
counterfeiting the action of an old woman, deliver'd
me, the knave constable had set me i' the stocks, i'
the common stocks, for a witch.

*M.Q.*Sir, let me speak with you in your chamber, you
shall hear how things go, and, I warrant, to your
content.   Here is a letter will say somewhat.   Good
hearts, what ado here is to bring you together!
Sure, one of you does not serve heaven well, that 120
you are so cross'd.

Fal. Come up into my chamber.   *Exeunt*

Enter Fenton and Host

Ho. Master Fenton, talk not to me, my mind is heavy : **I**
will give over all.

Fen. Yet hear me speak.   Assist me in my purpose,
And (as I am a gentleman) I 'll give thee
A hundred pound in gold, more than your loss.

Ho. I will hear you, Master Fenton, and I will (at the
least) keep your counsel.

Fen. From time to time I have acquainted you
　　　With the dear love I bear to fair Anne Page,
　　　Who, mutually, hath answer'd my affection,　　　10
　　　(So far forth as herself might be her chooser)
　　　Even to my wish : I have a letter from her
　　　Of such contents as you will wonder at ;
　　　The mirth whereof, so larded with my matter,
　　　That neither singly can be manifested
　　　Without the show of both ; fat Falstaff
　　　Hath a great scene : the image of the jest
　　　I 'll show you here at large.　Hark, good mine host.
　　　To-night at Herne's oak, just 'twixt twelve and one,
　　　Must my sweet Nan present the Fairy Queen ;　　　20
　　　The purpose why, is here : in which disguise,
　　　While other jests are something rank on foot,
　　　Her father hath commanded her to slip
　　　Away with Slender, and with him at Eton
　　　Immediately to marry : she hath consented :
　　　Now, sir,
　　　Her mother (ever strong against that match
　　　And firm for Doctor Caius) hath appointed
　　　That he shall likewise shuffle her away,
　　　While other sports are tasking of their minds,　　　30
　　　And at the deanery, where a priest attends,
　　　Straight marry her : to this her mother's plot

She seemingly obedient likewise hath
Made promise to the doctor.   Now, thus it rests:
Her father means she shall be all in white;
And in that habit, when Slender sees his time
To take her by the hand, and bid her go,
She shall go with him: her mother hath intended,
(The better to denote her to the doctor,
For they must all be mask'd, and vizarded)   40
That quaint in green she shall be loose enrob'd,
With ribands pendent, flaring 'bout her head;
And when the doctor spies his vantage ripe,
To pinch her by the hand, and on that token,
The maid hath given consent to go with him.

Ho. Which means she to deceive? father, or mother?

Fen. Both, my good host, to go along with me:
And here it rests, that you 'll procure the vicar
To stay for me at church, 'twixt twelve and one,
And in the lawful name of marrying,   50
To give our hearts united ceremony.

Ho. Well, husband your device; I 'll to the vicar:
Bring you the maid, you shall not lack a priest.

Fen. So shall I evermore be bound to thee;
Besides, I 'll make a present recompence.   *Exeunt*

Act Fifth

SCENE I

A room in the Garter Inn

Enter Falstaff and Mistress Quickly

Fal. Prithee no more prattling ; go. I'll hold. This
is the third time ; I hope good luck lies in odd
numbers. Away! go. They say there is divinity
in odd numbers, either in nativity, chance, or death.
Away !

M.Q. I'll provide you a chain, and I'll do what I can
to get you a pair of horns.

Fal. Away, I say, time wears, hold up your head, and
mince.   *Exit Mrs Quickly*

Enter Ford

How now, Master Brook ? Master Brook, the   10
matter will be known to-night, or never. Be you
in the Park about midnight, at Herne's oak, and
you shall see wonders.

Fo. Went you not to her yesterday, sir, as you told me
you had appointed ?

Fal. I went to her, Master Brook, as you see, like a poor

old man, but I came from her, Master Brook, like a poor old woman. That same knave, Ford her husband, hath the finest mad devil of jealousy in him, Master Brook, that ever govern'd frenzy. I 20 will tell you, he beat me grievously, in the shape of a woman; for in the shape of man, Master Brook, I fear not Goliath with a weaver's beam, because I know also, life is a shuttle. I am in haste, go along with me, I'll tell you all, Master Brook. Since I pluck'd geese, play'd truant, and whipp'd top, I knew not what 'twas to be beaten, till lately. Follow me, I'll tell you strange things of this knave Ford, on whom to-night I will be reveng'd, and I will deliver his wife into your hand. Follow; 30 strange things in hand, Master Brook! Follow.

Exeunt

SCENES II TO V

Windsor Park

Enter Page, Shallow, and Slender

Pa. Come, come; we'll couch i' the castle-ditch, till we see the light of our fairies. Remember, son Slender, my daughter.

Sle. Ay, forsooth, I have spoke with her, and we have
a nay-word, how to know one another : I come to
her in white, and cry, ' mum ; ' she cries ' budget,' †
and by that we know one another.

Sha. That 's good too : but what needs either your
' mum,' or her ' budget ? ' the white will decipher
her well enough.   It hath struck ten o'clock.   10

Pa. The night is dark, light and spirits will become it
well.   Heaven prosper our sport !   No man means
evil but the devil, and we shall know him by his
horns.   Let 's away ; follow me.   *Exeunt*

Enter Mistress Page, Mistress Ford, and Doctor Caius

M.P. Master Doctor, my daughter is in green : when
you see your time, take her by the hand, away with
her to the deanery, and dispatch it quickly : go
before into the Park : we two must go together.

Cai. I know vat I have to do, adieu.

M.P. Fare you well, sir. (*exit Caius.*) My husband will
not rejoice so much at the abuse of Falstaff, as he
will chafe at the doctor's marrying my daughter :

but 'tis no matter; better a little chiding, than a
great deal of heart-break.   10

M.F. Where is Nan now? and her troop of fairies? and
the Welsh devil?   †

M.P. They are all crouch'd in a pit hard by Herne's oak,
with obscur'd lights; which, at the very instant of
Falstaff's and our meeting, they will at once display
to the night.

M.F. That cannot choose but amaze him.

M.P. If he be not amaz'd, he will be mock'd; if he be
amaz'd, he will every way be mock'd.

M.F. We 'll betray him finely.   20

M.P. Against such lewdsters, and their lechery,
Those that betray them do no treachery.

M.F. The hour draws on.   To the oak, to the oak!

Exeunt

Enter Sir Hugh Evans disguised, with others as Fairies

Ev. Trib, trib, fairies; come; and remember your
parts: be pold, I pray you, follow me into the
pit, and when I give the watch-'ords, do as I pid
you: come, come, trib, trib.   *Exeunt*

Enter Falstaff disguised as Herne

Fal. The Windsor bell hath struck twelve; the minute
draws on. Now, the hot-blooded gods assist me!
Remember, Jove, thou wast a bull for thy Europa,
love set on thy horns. O powerful love, that, in
some respects, makes a beast a man; in some other,
a man a beast. You were also, Jupiter, a swan,
for the love of Leda. O omnipotent Love, how
near the god drew to the complexion of a goose! A
fault done first in the form of a beast;—O Jove,
a beastly fault! And then another fault, in the   10
semblance of a fowl;—think on 't, Jove; a foul
fault! When gods have hot backs, what shall poor
men do? For me, I am here a Windsor stag, and
the fattest, I think, i' the forest. Send me a cool
rut-time, Jove, or who can blame me to piss my
tallow?—Who comes here? my doe?

Enter Mistress Ford and Mistress Page

M.F. Sir John! art thou there, my deer? my male deer?

Fal. My doe, with the black scut? Let the sky rain
potatoes; let it thunder to the tune of Green Sleeves,
hail kissing-comfits, and snow eringoes; let there   20
come a tempest of provocation, I will shelter me here.

*M.F.*Mistress Page is come with me, sweetheart.

Fal. Divide me like a brib'd buck, each a haunch : I
will keep my sides to myself, my shoulders for the
fellow of this walk ; and my horns I bequeath your
husbands. Am I a woodman, ha ? Speak I like
Herne the hunter ? Why, now is Cupid a child of
conscience, he makes restitution. As I am a true
spirit, welcome ! *Noise within*

*M.P.*Alas, what noise ?　　　　　　　　　　　　　　3○

*M.F.*Heaven forgive our sins !

Fal. What should this be ?

M.F. \
　　　 } Away, away !　　　　　　　　　*They run off*
M.P. /

Fal. I think the devil will not have me damn'd, lest the
oil that 's in me should set hell on fire ; he would
never else cross me thus.

Enter Sir Hugh Evans, disguised as before ; Pistol, as Hob-
*　　goblin ; Mistress Quickly, Anne Page, and others, as*
*　　Fairies, with tapers*

*M Q.*Fairies, black, grey, green, and white,
　　　You moonshine revellers, and shades of night,
　　　You orphan heirs of fixed destiny,　　　　　　　†
　　　Attend your office, and your quality.
　　　Crier Hobgoblin, make the fairy oyes.

Pis. Elves, list your names ; silence, you airy toys.

    Cricket, to Windsor chimneys shalt thou leap ;
    Where fires thou find'st unrak'd, and hearths unswept,
    There pinch the maids as blue as bilberry,
    Our radiant queen hates sluts, and sluttery.

Fal. They are fairies ; he that speaks to them shall die :
    I 'll wink, and couch : no man their works must eye.
                        Lies down upon his face

Ev. Where 's Bede ? Go you, and where you find a maid
    That ere she sleep has thrice her prayers said,   50
    Raise up the organs of her fantasy,
    Sleep she as sound as careless infancy,
    But those as sleep, and think not on their sins,
    Pinch them, arms, legs, backs, shoulders, sides, and
        shins.

M.Q. About, about ;
    Search Windsor Castle, elves, within, and out :
    Strew good luck, ouphs, on every sacred room ;
    That it may stand till the perpetual doom,
    In state as wholesome as in state 'tis fit,
    Worthy the owner, and the owner it.   60
    The several chairs of order look you scour
    With juice of balm, and every precious flower :
    Each fair instalment, coat, and several crest,
    With loyal blazon, evermore be blest !
    And nightly, meadow-fairies, look you sing,

   Like to the Garter's compass, in a ring :
   Th' expressure that it bears, green let it be,
   More fertile-fresh than all the field to see ;
   And *Honi soit qui mal y pense* write
   In emerald tufts, flowers purple, blue, and white ; 70
   Like sapphire, pearl, and rich embroidery,
   Buckled below fair knighthood's bending knee :
   Fairies use flowers for their charactery.
   Away, disperse : but till 'tis one o'clock,
   Our dance of custom, round about the oak
   Of Herne the hunter, let us not forget.
Ev. Pray you lock hand in hand ; yourselves in order set ;
   And twenty glow-worms shall our lanterns be,
   To guide our measure round about the tree.
   But, stay, I smell a man of middle-earth. 8o
Fal. Heavens defend me from that Welsh fairy, lest he
   transform me to a piece of cheese !
Pis. Vile worm, thou wast o'erlook'd even in thy birth.
M.Q. With trial-fire touch me his finger-end :
   If he be chaste, the flame will back descend,
   And turn him to no pain ; but if he start,
   It is the flesh of a corrupted heart.
Pis. A trial, come.
Ev   Come ; will this wood take fire ?
       They burn him with their tapers

Fal. Oh, Oh, Oh !

*M.Q.*Corrupt, corrupt, and tainted in desire !   90

About him, fairies, sing a scornful rhyme,

And as you trip, still pinch him to your time.

SONG

Fie on sinful fantasy !

Fie on lust, and luxury !

Lust is but a bloody fire,

Kindled with unchaste desire,

Fed in heart, whose flames aspire,

As thoughts do blow them higher and higher.

Pinch him, fairies, mutually ;

Pinch him for his villany ;   100

Pinch him, and burn him, and turn him about,

Till candles, and starlight, and moonshine be out.

*During this song they pinch Falstaff. Doctor Caius comes
one way, and steals away a boy in green ; Slender another
way, and takes off a boy in white ; and Fenton comes, and
steals away Mistress Anne Page. A noise of hunting
is heard within. All the Fairies run away. Falstaff
pulls off his buck's head, and rises*

Enter Page, Ford, Mistress Page, and Mistress Ford

Pa. Nay, do not fly, I think we have watch'd you now :

Will none but Herne the hunter serve your turn ?

*M.P.*I pray you, come, hold up the jest no higher.

115

Now, good Sir John, how like you Windsor wives?
See you these, husband? do not these fair yokes
Become the forest better than the town?

Fo. Now, sir, who's a cuckold now? Master Brook, Falstaff's a knave, a cuckoldy knave, here are his 110 horns, Master Brook: and, Master Brook, he hath enjoy'd nothing of Ford's but his buck-basket, his cudgel, and twenty pounds of money, which must be paid to Master Brook; his horses are arrested for it, Master Brook.

M.F. Sir John, we have had ill luck; we could never † meet. I will never take you for my love again, but I will always count you my deer.

Fal. I do begin to perceive that I am made an ass.

Fo. Ay, and an ox too: both the proofs are extant. 120

Fal. And these are not fairies: I was three or four times in the thought they were not fairies, and yet the guiltiness of my mind, the sudden surprise of my powers, drove the grossness of the foppery into a receiv'd belief, in despite of the teeth of all rhyme and reason, that they were fairies. See now how wit may be made a Jack-a-Lent, when 'tis upon ill employment!

Ev. Sir John Falstaff, serve Got, and leave your desires, and fairies will not pinse you. 130

Fo. Well said, fairy Hugh.

Ev. And leave you your jealousies too, I pray you.

Fo. I will never mistrust my wife again, till thou art able
to woo her in good English.

Fal. Have I laid my brain in the sun, and dried it, that it
wants matter to prevent so gross o'erreaching as
this ?   Am I ridden with a Welsh goat too ?   shall
I have a coxcomb of frieze ?   'Tis time I were chok'd
with a piece of toasted cheese.

Ev. Seese is not good to give putter ; your pelly is all 140
putter.

Fal. ' Seese ' and ' putter ' ?   Have I liv'd to stand at the
taunt of one that makes fritters of English ?   This
is enough to be the decay of lust and late-walking
through the realm.

M.P. Why, Sir John, do you think, though we would
have thrust virtue out of our hearts by the head and
shoulders, and have given ourselves without scruple
to hell, that ever the devil could have made you our
delight ?   150

Fo. What, a hodge-pudding ?   a bag of flax ?

M.P. A puff'd man ?

Pa. Old, cold, wither'd, and of intolerable entrails ?

Fo. And one that is as slanderous as Satan ?

Pa. And as poor as Job ?

Fo. And as wicked as his wife?

Ev. And given to fornications, and to taverns, and
sack, and wine, and metheglins, and to drinkings,
and swearings, and starings? pribbles and prabbles?

Fal. Well, I am your theme: you have the start of me, 160
I am dejected; I am not able to answer the Welsh
flannel: ignorance itself is a plummet o'er me: use
me as you will.

Fo. Marry, sir, we'll bring you to Windsor, to one
Master Brook, that you have cozen'd of money, to
whom you should have been a pandar: over and
above that you have suffer'd, I think, to repay that
money will be a biting affliction.

Pa. Yet be cheerful, knight: thou shalt eat a posset
to-night at my house, where I will desire thee to 170
laugh at my wife, that now laughs at thee: tell
her Master Slender hath married her daughter.

M.P.(aside) Doctors doubt that: if Anne Page be my
daughter, she is, by this, Doctor Caius' wife.

Enter Slender

Sle. Whoa, ho! ho, father Page!

Pa. Son, how now? how now, son? have you dispatch'd?

Sle. Dispatched? I'll make the best in Gloucestershire
know on 't: would I were hang'd, la, else!

Pa. Of what, son? 18c

Sle. I came yonder at Eton to marry Mistress Anne
Page, and she's a great lubberly boy. If it had
not been i' the church, I would have swing'd him,
or he should have swing'd me. If I did not think
it had been Anne Page, would I might never stir !—
and 'tis a postmaster's boy.

Pa. Upon my life, then, you took the wrong.

Sle. What need you tell me that? I think so, when I
took a boy for a girl. If I had been married to him,
for all he was in woman's apparel, I would not have 19c
had him.

Pa. Why, this is your own folly, did not I tell you how
you should know my daughter, by her garments?

Sle. I went to her in white, and cried ' mum,' and she
cried ' budget,' as Anne and I had appointed, and
yet it was not Anne, but a postmaster's boy.

M.P. Good George, be not angry, I knew of your
purpose ; turn'd my daughter into green ; and,
indeed, she is now with the doctor at the deanery,
and there married. 200

Enter Caius

Cai. Vere is Mistress Page? By gar, I am cozen'd : I
ha' married un garçon, a boy ; un paysan, by gar :
a boy, it is not Anne Page, by gar, I am cozen'd.

119

*M.P.*Why, did you take her in green?

Cai. Ay, be gar, and 'tis a boy: be gar, I'll raise all
  Windsor.   *Exit*

Fo. This is strange. Who hath got the right Anne?

Pa. My heart misgives me:—here comes Master Fenton.

Enter Fenton and Anne Page

  How now, Master Fenton?

An. Pardon, good father; good my mother, pardon!   210

Pa. Now, mistress; how chance you went not with
  Master Slender?

*M.P.*Why went you not with master doctor, maid?

Fen. You do amaze her: hear the truth of it.
  You would have married her most shamefully,
  Where there was no proportion held in love.
  The truth is, she and I, long since contracted,
  Are now so sure that nothing can dissolve us.
  The offence is holy that she hath committed,
  And this deceit loses the name of craft,   220
  Of disobedience, or unduteous title,
  Since therein she doth evitate and shun
  A thousand irreligious cursed hours,
  Which forced marriage would have brought upon her.

Fo. Stand not amaz'd, here is no remedy:
  In love, the heavens themselves do guide the state,
  Money buys lands, and wives are sold by fate.

Fal. I am glad, though you have ta'en a special stand
　　　To strike at me, that your arrow hath glanc'd.
Pa. Well, what remedy?　Fenton, heaven give thee joy !　230
　　　What cannot be eschew'd must be embrac'd.
Fal. When night-dogs run, all sorts of deer are chas'd.
M.P. Well, I will muse no further.　Master Fenton,
　　　Heaven give you many, many merry days !
　　　Good husband, let us every one go home,
　　　And laugh this sport o'er by a country fire,
　　　Sir John and all.
Fo. 　　　　　　Let it be so.　Sir John,
　　　To Master Brook you yet shall hold your word,
　　　For he, to night, shall lie with Mistress Ford.

Exeunt

(*Appended is the conclusion, as given in Q, corresponding
to ll. 230-end of F.*)
　　　　　　　　　　　　　　　　　　　　　　　　　　　　†

[*M.F.* Come, Mistress Page, I will be bold with you,
　　　'Tis pity to part love that is so true.
M.P. Although that I have miss'd in my intent,
　　　Yet I am glad my husband's match was cross'd ;
　　　Here, Master Fenton, take her, and God give thee joy.
Ev. Come, Master Page, you must needs agree.
Fo. I' faith, sir, come, you see your wife 's well pleas'd.
Pa. I cannot tell, and yet my heart 's well eas'd,

And yet it doth me good the doctor miss'd.
Come hither, Fenton, and come hither, daughter ;
Go to, you might have stay'd for my good will,
But since your choice is made of one you love,
Here take her, Fenton, and both happy prove.

Ev. I will also dance and eat plums at your weddings.

Fo. All parties pleas'd, now let us in to feast,
And laugh at Slender, and the doctor's jest.
He hath got the maiden, each of you a boy
To wait upon you, so God give you joy ;
And, Sir John Falstaff, now shall you keep your word,
For Brook this night shall lie with Mistress Ford.]

Notes

I. i. 5-7. *Coram*, etc.; *Coram* is a common corruption (*i.e.* nothing to do with Slender's stupidity) of 'quorum,' the first word in the clause of the Commission which named the justices. *Custalorum* is for 'custos rotulorum,' 'the keeper of the rolls,' and *Ratolorum* Slender's blunder for the second word of the phrase.

I. i. 15. *dozen white luces*; here, and in the passage which follows, there are clear allusions to Sir Thomas Lucy, of Charlecote in Warwickshire. The Lucy arms were 'three luces argent in a shield gules.' There is a strong tradition, which may well enough be true, that Shakespeare as a young man fell foul of Sir Thomas Lucy over a deer-stealing escapade, and that in this passage he was taking a comparatively good-humoured revenge. But it is not necessary therefore to identify Shallow with Sir Thomas Lucy. *Louses* is, of course, merely Sir Hugh's blunder for *luces*.

I. i. 18. *passant*; the luces were in fact 'haurient,' *i.e.* vertical; but the louses are clearly more appropriate 'passant,' *i.e.* walking. I see no reason for taking the word as 'en passant,' which hardly fits the context; if we are to look for any other than the obvious heraldic meaning, I should assume a blunder of Sir Hugh's for 'passing,' *i.e.* 'passing well,' 'excellently well.'

I. i. 20. *the salt fish is an old coat*; there has been no adequate explanation of this. The New Cambridge editors suggest *cod* for *coat*, on the assumption that Shallow thought that Sir Hugh meant 'cod' by 'coat.' But why should he think so, when Sir Hugh's remark makes admirable sense as it stands, and little, if any, sense with 'cod'?

I. i. 38. *sword*; the New Cambridge editors would read *swort* with a play on *sort* (='upshot'). (?) *word*.

I. i. 53, 55. *Slender*; Capell gave both speeches to Shallow. The remarks are not particularly typical of Slender, but there seems neither necessity nor authority for the change. The New Cambridge editors comment, "*N.B.*—The second speech cannot be Slender's after his words at ll. 43, 44." But why, because he implies there that he knows her appearance, should he not be allowed to say again that he knows her?

I. i. 105. *But not kiss'd your keeper's daughter*; this looks like a topical allusion.

I. i. 163. A mysterious speech of Bardolph's. To begin with, *fap* is not found again till 1818, and then probably taken from this passage. If correct, it is presumably a slang word for 'drunk.' In the second place *pass the car-eires* (so F), if *car-eires*='careers,' is no doubt a technical term from horsemanship, but what *conclusions passed the careers* means has not been explained, even if *conclusions* is merely Bardolph's blunder for 'in conclusion.' Finally, Slender rather implies that Bardolph is speaking Latin, though this may mean no more than that he does not understand Bardolph's argot.

I. i. 180. *Book of Songs and Sonnets*; i.e. the Earl of Surrey's *Songs and Sonnets* (1557), the real 'best-seller' of the day, in fact what we know as *Tottel's Miscellany*.

I. i. 218. *carry-her*; hyphened, as in F. Is there some point in *car-eires* and *carry-her* that we have lost?

I. i. 231. *content*; so F, but universally emended to *contempt*. Slender, however, is bound to make a blunder either way. If he says *content* he garbles the proverb and says what he means; if he says *contempt* he gets the proverb right but says the opposite of what he means. And there seems no reason for meddling with F merely to give Slender a different blunder.

I. iii. 19. *Hungarian*; Q reads *Gongarian*, and Steevens exasperatingly records that he remembers in one of the old bombast plays a line, *O base Gongarian, wilt thou the distaff wield?*, but that he forgot to note it.

I. iii. 27. *minute's*; Langton conjectures *minim's*; the New Cambridge editors warmly support this, reading *minim-rest*.

I. iii. 46. *studied her will*; Q reads *well* for *will*, and this may be right. Many conjectures, *well . . . well, well . . . will, well . . . ill*.

I. iii. 50. *legend*; so F. Q reads *legions*; we should perhaps read *legion*, since Falstaff's humour almost never depends on a Quicklyan derangement of epitaphs.

I. iii. 71. *Pandarus*; Q reads *Panderowes*. Is this merely an amusing auditory error, or does it represent Pistol's mispronunciation? And has it any connection with the Q reading *randevowes*, where F reads *harvest-home* (II. ii. 268)?

I. iii. 80. *French thrift*; the allusion, as Hart points out, is doubtless to the contemporary employment of French pages and the discarding of a superfluity of serving-men. And *skirted*, at its face value, means just 'wearing a coat with skirts,' but the capital (as in F, which also italicises) helps to point Falstaff's pun on Mistress Page.

I. iii. 88. *By welkin, and her star*; Q reads *By Welkin and her Fairies*. Greg is probably right in thinking that this reading means no more than that the reporter misunderstood *Welkin* as the name of a witch and thought that fairies were appropriate; but it is an odd reading, which one may perhaps suspect of concealing an error of Nym's rather than the reporter's. As it stands it means of course merely 'by the sky and the sun (or moon, or morning-star) in it.'

I. iii. 97. *yellows*; Q *Iallowes*, F *yallownesse*. Q seems much the more vigorous.

I. iv. 20. *whey face*; F reads *wee-face*; *with a little yellow Beard; a Caine colour'd Beard*. Q reads *whay coloured beard* and *kane colored* (though the speeches are jumbled and there is nothing about his face). I think that Q has preserved the true reading. *Wee* is redundant, apart from being uncommon in the south till later, and nowhere else used by Shakespeare. *Whey* (in this context) is no doubt also uncommon, but it is at least Shakespearean (*Macbeth*, V. iii. 17).

I. iv. 103. *it is a shallenge*; Q reads *it ber ve chalenge*. (?) *it be-a ve challenge*.

I. iv. 120. *An fool's-head*; it is clear from F, which prints *An* not only here but for the two following *Anne's*, that a pun is intended, though it is not an obvious one. It means, I suppose, 'made a fool of by your disappointed aspirations for Anne.'

II. i. 5. *precisian*; so F (Q gives no help). Johnson's emendation of *Physician* has a certain attractiveness and is supported by Sonnet 147. But it is hard to see why so ordinary a word as *physician* should have been misread, and the F reading may well stand; 'love allows reason to preach at him, but does not follow his advice.'

II. i. 114. *Like Sir Actæon he*; I see no reason for emending *he* to *be*. This use of *he* is common enough in ballad. Actæon, in Greek myth, was a hunter who, having seen Artemis naked, was changed into a stag, and run down and killed by his own hounds; but he became to the Elizabethans, with their insistence, not to say their damnably wearisome iteration, on the horns as a symbol of cuckoldry, a type of the 'horned' cuckold.

II. i. 120. *Away sir.* . . . . F reads *Away sir Corporall* Nim: *Beleeve it* (Page) *he speakes sence.* Q reads *Page believe him what he ses. Away sir Corporall Nym.* The New Cambridge editors, believing that F's '(Page)' is a stage-direction that has crept into the text, read *Away, Sir Corporal Nym* . . . (to Page) *Believe it, he speaks sense*; and this has the undoubted merit of making a six-foot line. But I think that with the punctuation of the text a good enough sense is given. Pistol, as he turns to go, as it were introduces Nym to Page with a testimonial.

II. i. 204. *An-heires*; much conjecture. Theobald tried *Mynheers*; Hart, very plausibly, *Ameers* (probably in the form *Amyras*). It pretty certainly conceals a specimen of the Host's love for high-sounding titles. (But may it be nothing more than his usual *Cavaleiros*, unless from this and *car-eires* with the same odd hyphen we should suspect some lost topical hit.)

II. ii. 25. *yet you, you rogue*; F reads *yet, you rogue*; Q *yet you stand upon your honor, you rogue*; it is easy simply to shift F's comma, as is usually done, and read *yet you, rogue*, but I think that the insertion of the easily dropped second *you* gives a more natural emphasis.

II. ii. 132. *punk*; Warburton's emendation to *pink* is most attractive. A *pink* is a fishing vessel.

II. ii. 265. *wittolly*; *wittol* is a contraction of 'wudewale'=green finch, in whose nest, according to mediæval ornithologists, the cuckoo laid its eggs: this connection led to its becoming a cant term for cuckold.

II. iii. 24. *punto*, etc.; various fencing terms. The *punto* and *stock* are straightforward thrusts; the *montant* an upward thrust; and the *reverse* a back-handed stroke (implying both edge and point work).

II. iii. 28. *bully-stale*; this odd word seems to be connected with the diuretic jokes of ll. 31 and 54, which (like others elsewhere, *e.g.* 2 *Henry IV*, I. ii. 1) were based on medical practice of the time.

II. iii. 54. *Mock-water*; the joke is entirely obscure, and no comments really illuminate it, and emendations to either *Make-water* or *Muck-water*, though they emphasise the nature of the joke, do not make its point any clearer. One rather suspects some topical allusion to a proper name known at the time (presumably a ' Mac ' name, like the ' very valiant ' Macmorris of *Henry V*).

II. iii. 79. *Let him die*; there is no need, I think, to insert after these words *but first* from Q. The Host means ' Don't bother about killing him ; let him die as he will, and meantime come with me to more attractive business.'

II. iii. 83. *Cried-game*; F reads *wooe her : Cride-game*; Q *wear hir cried game.* Against this coincidence any emendation (the usual one is *Cried I aim*) is dangerous. And the suggestion that *Cried game* is some slang insult of the Host's is surely improbable, since for the moment the Host and Caius are striking up an alliance (even though it is true that the Host might deliver an insult which Caius would not understand). It is probably some sporting term. (Other possibilities are that we should stick to Q and suppose that *Cried game* conceals some ' favour ' of Anne's ; or that the Host is airing his French in some phrase which appears as *Cride* (or *Cried*) *game*.)

III. i. 16. *To shallow rivers*; Sir Hugh is misquoting a popular song by Marlowe.

III. ii. 63. *buttons*; Hart interprets as ' he has it in him.' But Q's reading *betmes*, meaningless as it is, should have attention paid to it, since it is in a speech of the Host. (If one could account for the *be* of *betmes*, it would be tempting to read *lines*, *i.e.* ' fortune ').

III. iii. 36. *Have I . . .* ; the line is from Sidney's *Astrophel and Stella*. Q may be right in omitting *thee*, but the insertion, adapting the quotation to the circumstances, is natural enough.

III. iii. 53. *By the Lord, thou art a traitor*; so Q. F reads, surprisingly, *Thou art a tyrant*. Even the rigidly conservative Hart admits Q without a tremor and almost without a comment, while equally surprisingly the New Cambridge editors hold on to *tyrant*.

III. iii. 57. F punctuates *If Fortune thy foe, were not Nature thy friend*. The sense is clear, ' if Fortune were not thy foe and only Nature thy friend,' or ' if only Fortune, at present thy foe, were as much thy friend as Nature is.'

III. iii. 64, 69. *Bucklersbury . . . Counter-gate*. Bucklersbury was a London street with many apothecaries' shops, which were fragrant at the time when the fresh simples were brought in. Countergate was a debtor's prison, near Bucklersbury, notorious for its smell. The New Cambridge editors see, perhaps rightly, a pun on ' counter-gait.'

III. iii. 151. *uncape*; the New Cambridge editors make the attractive suggestion *uncope* (*i.e.* ' unmuzzle the ferrets ').

III. iv. 40. *two geese out of a pen*; so F. Q reads *the goose out of the henloft*. Though neither story sounds exactly a ' rib-binder,' the Q version suggests more hilarious possibilities.

IV. ii. 17. *lines*; so F. (Q *vaine*.) Usually emended to *lunes*, but the parallels adduced are, as Hart pointed out, themselves mostly emendations and of the flimsiest authority. *Line* has so many vague usages, some of them (and notably the modern American colloquial usage) close to the sense here needed, that emendation is unnecessary.

IV. iii. This scene, with IV. v. 59-87, is almost all that is left of the horse-stealing sub-plot, for a brilliant reconstruction of which see Hart's introduction to the play in the Arden edition.

IV. iv. 27. *Herne*; It is tempting to follow the New Cambridge editors in preferring Q's *Horne* to F's *Herne* throughout. It gives an additional point to l. 42 and F, which reads the pointless *Broome* throughout for Q's *Brooke* (as Ford's alias; is this possibly some Oldcastle-Falstaff trouble over some actual Windsor citizen?), is no authority on proper names. But the point is hardly important enough to make one desert the familiar traditional reading.

IV. v. 50. *Ay, tyke . . .*; so Q (*I tike, who more bold*). F reads *I Sir : like who more bold.* Farmer combined the readings, *Ay, Sir Tyke; who more bold?* Hart stigmatises it as a grotesque reading. I prefer the grotesque to the meaningless.

IV. v. 72. *cozen-germans*; Q reads *cosen garmombles*; this is the clearest relic of 'the Mümpelgart business' that was the foundation of the horse-stealing plot.

V. ii. 6. *mum . . . budget*; *mum* is a common word for silence ('mum's the word,' etc.); but *mumbudget* as a whole means much the same; 'to play mumbudget' is 'to be tongue-tied.'

V. iii. 12. *Welsh devil?* This is Hart's reading. F reads *Welch-devill Herne.* As Hart suggests, *Herne* may have crept in from the line below. Most editors emend to *Hugh.* The New Cambridge editors read *devil-hern*, on the grounds that in Q's stage-direction Sir Hugh enters 'like a Satyre' and that he is therefore *devil-hern* in two senses, (*a*) as to his head (hern=brain), and (*b*) because he is to 'devil' Herne. I do not feel this convincing (the fact that 'hern'='brain' does not make it equal 'head'), and if we are to emend I would rather go further and transpose to *horne-devil.*

V. iv. 3-12. Jupiter wooed Europa in the form of a bull and Leda in that of a swan.

V. v. 39. *orphan heirs*; if orphan is correct the New Cambridge editors are probably right in connecting it with the superstition that fairies are the souls of dead children (though that is not the same as orphan children). But Theobald's *ouphen* is tempting.

V. v. 116. *we could never meet*; the New Cambridge editors comment that their emendation *mate* " seems self-evident! They had ' met ' three times, but never ' mated.' " The emendation is easily justified on grounds of spelling and pronunciation, but it seems to miss the ironic point of Mistress Ford's remark. No doubt we should now naturally say, ' Why, we're always meeting,' but the text as it stands is the exact equivalent of the American idiom, ' Isn't it too bad we can't ever meet? ' which means the opposite of what it says.

V. v. 239. I have appended the concluding lines of the play as they are given in Q. They are an interesting example of Q at its best. There are a few roughnesses, but in general the conclusion seems more rounded and neater than that of F. It gives both the Fords, both the Pages, and Sir Hugh their say, it summarises the failure of Slender and Caius, and it clinches the play with an admirable couplet.

Glossary

MANY words and phrases in Shakespeare require glossing, not because they are in themselves unfamiliar, but for the opposite reason, that Shakespeare uses in their Elizabethan and unfamiliar sense a large number of words which seem so familiar that there is no incentive to look for them in the glossary. It is hoped that a glossary arranged as below will make it easy to see at a glance what words and phrases in any particular scene require elucidation. A number of phrases are glossed by what seems to be, in their context, the modern equivalent rather than by lexicographical glosses on the words which compose them.

Act First

SCENE I

line

1 STARCHAMBER, high court of justice

8 'ARMIGERO,' *i.e.* knight

15 LUCES, pikes

21 QUARTER, combine two coats of arms

30 ATONEMENTS, reconcilements

35 TAKE YOUR VIZAMENTS IN THAT, 'you may lay to that'

44 SMALL, high-pitched

81 FALLOW, pale-brown

82 COTSALL, Cotswold

113 WORTS, *pun on* (a) *words*, (b) *plants*

116 CONY-CATCHING, cheating

142 GROAT, 4d.

line

142 MILL-SIXPENCE, 6d. struck in a mill

143 SHOVEL-BOARDS, silver shillings used for 'shove-halfpenny'

148 LATTEN, soft metal
BILBO, sword

149 LABRAS, lips

153 NUTHOOK, constable, 'cop'

158 SCARLET, JOHN, *i.e.* Robin Hood's Will Scarlet and Little John

261 VENEYS, bouts

262 STEW'D PRUNES, 'a recognised dish of prostitutes,' *and so came to be a cant term for* prostitutes

Act I   Sc. i—*continued*

line
262 WARD, guard
263 HOT, hit
272 SACKERSON, a famous bear
274 PASS'D, 'was the limit'

line
279 COCK AND PIE, 'cock' is corruption of 'God,' and 'pie' i. the Roman Catholic ordinal

SCENE II

4 LAUNDRY, laundress

12 PIPPINS, apples

SCENE III

2 ROOK, (*a*) sharper, (*b*) castle (at chess): *perhaps therefore a relic of a stage when Falstaff was Oldcastle*
6 WAG, 'buzz off'
10 ENTERTAIN, give a job to
14 FROTH, make frothy
LIME, put lime in (*to reduce sourness*)
AT A WORD, laconic
22 HUMOUR, *it is impossible to gloss all the shades of meaning of Nym's favourite word; trick is often the nearest equivalent*

28 FICO, fig
31 KIBES, sores on heel
32 CONY-CATCH, cheat
42 CARVES, (?) speaks affectedly
50 LEGEND, *i.e.* legion
ANGELS, coins
56 ŒILLADES, glances of eye
66 CHEATERS, escheaters, officers of exchequer
81 GOURD AND FULLAM, false dice
83 TESTER, coin
94 PROVE, tempt
97 YELLOWS, jaundice

SCENE IV

4 OLD, 'rare'
7 POSSET, hot drink
8 SEA-COAL, sea-borne coal (*as distinct from local charcoal*)
11 BREED-BATE, quarrel-breeder

18 GLOVER'S PARING-KNIFE, crescent-shaped knife
22 SOFTLY-SPRIGHTED, gently-spirited
25 WARRENER, gamekeeper

Act I Sc. iv—*continued*

line
34 SHENT, scolded
41 TOYS, trifles
47 HORN-MAD, stark-mad
60 SIMPLES, medicinal herbs

line
106 STONES, testicles
116 WHAT, THE GOOD-JER, 'a meaningless expletive'

Act Second

SCENE I

5 PRECISIAN, preacher
23 UNWEIGH'D, light
24 PICK'D, inferred
CONVERSATION, behaviour
28 EXHIBIT, submit
34 ILL, (*a*) cross, (*b*) 'poorly'
49 HACK, *many conjectures, no explanation, see N.E.D.*
60 'GREEN SLEEVES,' the tune of 'an amorous ballad' which came to have some association with prostitutes
78 TURTLES, doves

106 CURTAL, dock-tailed
111 GALLIMAUFRY, hotch-potch
114 RINGWOOD, name of hound (*cf.* '*John Peel*')
137 CATAIAN, *i.e.* Cathayan = Chinese = (*apparently*) liar
163 YOKE, pair
181 BULLY-ROOK, see gloss on I. iii. 2
200 SACK, white wine of sherry type
209 STOCCADOES, thrust at fencing
214 WAG, 'buzz off'
217 SECURE, care-free

SCENE II

1 RETORT, repay
IN EQUIPAGE, in instalments
6 GRATED UPON, worried
9 GRATE, prison-bars
GEMINY, pair
11 TALL FELLOWS, 'stout fellows'
18 SHORT KNIFE AND A THRONG, *the desideranda for the cutpurse*
25 LURCH, lurk

26 CAT-A-MOUNTAIN, wild-cat
27 RED-LATTICE, 'pot-house talk' (Onions)
59 CANARY, *properly* a quick Spanish dance
70 ANGELS, coins
75 PENSIONERS, the Queen's bodyguard (selected from men of rank)

Act II Sc. ii—*continued*

line
88 FRAMPOLD, cross-grained
123 NAY-WORD, pass-word
132 PUNK, bawd
150 VIA! away!
191 ENGROSS'D, seized
217 SHREWD CONSTRUCTION, acid comment
220 ADMITTANCE, entrée
240 INSTANCE, evidence
241 WARD, guard
271 MECHANICAL, low-class
SALT-BUTTER, *i.e.* poor

line
277 AGGRAVATE HIS STYLE, give him an extra name
280 EPICUREAN, voluptuous
291 ADDITIONS, names
293 SECURE (*free from anxiety, i.e.*) blind
298 AMBLING, an easy gait of a horse, distinguished from the trot by the fore and hind legs of the same side moving together

SCENE III

22 FOIN, thrust
TRAVERSE, move sideways
26-7 ÆSCULAPIUS, GALEN, old physicians
HEART OF ELDER, *i.e.* mere pith (*for the expected 'heart of oak'*)

37 HAIR, 'against the grain' (*from rubbing fur the wrong way*)
61 CLAPPER-CLAW, maul
66 WAG, 'buzz off'

Act Third

SCENE I

5 PITTIE-WARD, *meaning unexplained*
14 COSTARD, head
56 WIDE OF HIS OWN RESPECT, far from his reputation

63 HIBOCRATES, *i.e.* Hippocrates, an old physician
114 SCALL, scoundrelly
115 COGGING, cheating

SCENE II

line		*line*	
30	TWELVE SCORE, *sc.* paces (*the full length of an archery range*)	46	KNOT, crowd
38	DIVULGE, disclose	66	HAVING, substance
39	ACTÆON, see note on II. i. 114	82	CANARY, wine from the Canaries
40	CRY AIM, applaud	83	PIPE-WINE, wine from the cask (*with pun on 'dance'*)

SCENE III

2	BUCK-BASKET, clothes-basket	78	PRESENTLY, at once
12	WHITSTERS, bleachers	112	STAND, delay
19	EYAS-MUSKET, young male sparrow-hawk	118	BUCKING, bleaching
22	JACK-A-LENT, 'Aunt Sally'	133	COWL-STAFF, pole through the two handles
34	PUMPION, water-melon		DRUMBLE, loiter
35	TURTLES, doves (*type of constancy, as jays of flightiness*)	143	WASH MYSELF OF THE BUCK, *i.e.* get rid of my 'horns'
40	COG, cheat	151	UNCAPE, disclose
49	SHIP-TIRE, ETC., various fanciful coiffures	171	GROSS, blatant
51	BECOME, are suited by	175	OBEY, yield to
56	FARTHINGALE, hooped skirt	192	PRESSES, cupboards

SCENE IV

5	GALL'D, damaged	62	HAPPY MAN BE HIS DOLE, good luck to him !
	EXPENSE, extravagance	84	QUICK, alive
7	BARS, objections		
46	COME CUT AND LONG-TAIL, whoever comes (*properly 'docked or otherwise'*)		

SCENE V

line		line	
3	TOAST, piece of toast	101	BELL-WETHER, ram with bell to lead the flock
9	SLIGHTED, (?) slid	102	BILBO, sword
22	REINS, innards	103	PECK, cylindrical measure
65	PEAKING, prying	105	FRETTED, fermented
	CORNUTO, cuckold	114	GOOD SADNESS, sober earnest
101	WITH, by	142	HORN-MAD, stark-mad

Act Fourth

SCENE I

line		line	
47	CARET, is lacking	74	SPRAG, *i.e.* sprack = quick
71	PREECHES, *i.e.* 'breeched' = whipped		

SCENE II

line		line	
1	EATEN UP, wiped out	149	LEMAN, paramour
	SUFFERANCE, suffering	161	FIGURE, horoscope
2	OBSEQUIOUS, devoted		DAUBERY, chicanery
50	KILN-HOLE, fire-hole of a kiln	168	POLECAT, *term of abuse*, (?) prostitute
52	PRESS, cupboard		
54	ABSTRACT, summary	169	RONYON, *term of abuse*
69	THRUMM'D, fringed	192	FEE-SIMPLE . . . RECOVERY, law terms for absolute possession
82	GOOD SADNESS, sober earnest		
96	DRAFF, husks	196	FIGURES, delusions
108	GING, gang	202	PERIOD, end
112	THIS PASSES, 'this is the limit'		

SCENE IV

line
31 TAKES, malignantly charms
35 ELD, people of old
49 OUPH, goblin child
54 DIFFUSED, scattered
UPON THEIR SIGHT, the moment we see them

line
67 JACK-AN-APES, devil
70 VIZARDS, masks
77 PROPERTIES, disguises
78 TRICKING, adorning

SCENE V

6 STANDING-BED, fixed bed
TRUCKLE-BED, movable bed
8 ANTHROPOPHAGINIAN, cannibal
16 EPHESIAN, boon-companion
26 MUSSEL-SHELL, (? one who gapes, *but most probably simply*) worthless person

50 TYKE, cur
65 FAUSTUS, *sold his soul to the devil*
72 COZEN'D, cheated
96 PRIMERO, card-game

SCENE VI

14 LARDED, sandwiched
22 RANK ON FOOT, ' going strong '
42 FLARING, streaming

55 PRESENT RECOMPENCE, reward on the nail

Act Fifth

SCENE III

17 AMAZE, bemuse

SCENE V

18 SCUT, tail
19 GREEN SLEEVES, see gloss on II. i. 60

20 KISSING-COMFIT, cachou
ERINGOES, candied sea-holly (*regarded as an aphrodisiac*)

Act V Sc. v—*continued*

line
23 BRIB'D, (?) stolen
41 OYES, town-crier's cry
57 OUPH, goblin child
66 COMPASS, circle
80 MIDDLE-EARTH, earth (*an old word implying the position between heaven and hell*)

line
94 LUXURY, lasciviousness
107 YOKES, horns
120 OX, *i.e.* 'horned'
138 COXCOMB, fool's cap
151 HODGE-PUDDING, hodge-podge
158 METHEGLINS, a kind of mead
222 EVITATE, avoid